POWER

OF THE

TONGUE

Bill Winston

Power of The Tongue
ISBN 1-931289-40-9
Copyright © 2002 Bill Winston
Bill Winston Ministries
P.O. Box 947
Oak Park, Illinois 60303-0947

Contents

Introduction

When I was living on Chicago's north side some years ago, one bitterly cold, winter day my car would not start. The wind-chill was about 60°C below zero. I was parked over on Inner Lake Shore Drive. When I got in my car and tried to start it, nothing happened. In fact, a lot of cars did not start. I noticed a tow truck driver cruising the street making all kinds of money starting cars. I said, "I'm not going to let him start my car." So what did I do? I got out of my car and as I stepped back, I looked around to see if anybody was watching me. Then I spoke to the car saying, "Car, in the Name of Jesus of Nazareth, I command you to start." Then I went inside and got a cup of hot chocolate to give God a chance to work. When I came back out and put my key in that ignition, the car started up just like it was a 70°C day.

This is just one of many examples in my life of how the words I have spoken in faith manifested in the natural realm. The first time you do something like this it looks foolish. Now, if I had been out there on the side of the highway kicking and cussing a stalled car, most people would have found my behavior more "normal." Many times when you step back from a crisis and speak God's Word over it, people will start pointing at you and calling you crazy—even some church folks. But God said to me, "You have been created in My image and likeness. The things that I do, you shall do also."

Jesus understood the power of His words. He spoke to a fig tree and it obeyed Him. He spoke to a storm and it obeyed Him. He spoke to a man who had been dead four days and stinking, and he obeyed Him. So, when my car would not start, it was time for me to speak and I did. This was not a coincidence. The Word worked just like God said it would and it will work for whosoever believes.

I did not start my Christian walk with this kind of faith. I learned it through the Word of God and through experience. I was timid at first. But as I studied God's Word and saw how He watches over His Word to perform it, my faith grew. As my faith grew, my confidence in speaking the Word over any situation also grew. I have learned to live by the Word of God and practice aligning my speech with His Word. The Bible is very clear on this subject and contains much wisdom about the power of the tongue.

A Matter of Life and Death

Death and life are in the power of the tongue: and they that love it shall eat the fruit thereof. [Proverbs 18:21]

Since you spend every waking moment trying to live, your tongue needs to line up with the life God has designed for you. This means you must learn to speak the promise not the problem. Understanding the power of words is the key to your destiny. Death and life are not in the power of the devil or in your pocketbook—but of the tongue.

A man's belly shall be satisfied with the fruit of his mouth; and with the increase of his lips shall he be filled. [Proverbs 18:20]

All increase comes by the tongue—by the words you speak. Words can also be the trigger for negative life experiences. Sometimes life situations can be the result of what someone else has said to you, which you receive and accept as valid. For example, someone may say, "You have a temper just like your father." Later, when you get angry, you try to excuse it by saying, "Well, they always said I had a temper just like my father." So when they say this and you repeat it, you are confirming a negative word. Thank God the spiritual law also works on the positive side, too. Therefore, words are the key to making life work. Proverbs 13:2-3 describes it well:

A man shall eat good by the fruit of his mouth: but the soul of the transgressors shall eat violence. He that keepeth his mouth keepeth his life: but he that openeth wide his lips shall have destruction.

Without a doubt, your words are connected to your life. Proverbs 10:11 makes the same point: *"The mouth of a righteous man is a well of life: but violence covereth the mouth of the wicked."* In Hebrew, the word *well* means "source." The connection between your words and your life is abundantly clear from these passages. The problem is that most people have not truly acknowledged the connection between what they say, what they have, and what they experience. This is because the revelation of this connection was lost in the Fall of man. But Jesus came to bring us back to this knowledge as part of the salvation experience.

CHAPTER ONE

Talk Like God Talks

> *The Spirit of the LORD spake by me, and his word was in my tongue.*
>
> 2 Samuel 23:2

God has invested a lot in your mouth. He put the power of life and death in your tongue—in your speech. Notice the Proverbs 18:21 passage cited previously does not read, "Death and life are in the power of God." We know God's power is the ultimate power. He entrusted you with the ability to exert power through speech. So you can speak life to your life or situation or you can speak death to it. Your words can take you over or take you under. Simply put, you can change your future by changing your words. You have the ability to do this because you are a child of God. In Romans 8:16-17 and Galatians 4:7, Christians are referred to as sons and joint-heirs. God as your Father set the standard as to how His sons and daughters are to live.

In the beginning God created the heaven and the earth. And the earth was without form, and void; and darkness was upon the face of the deep. And the Spirit of God moved upon the face of the waters. And God said, Let there be light: and there was light. [Genesis 1:1-3]

You will notice although the Holy Spirit was moving upon the face of the waters, nothing was happening. God was God; the Holy Spirit was the Holy Spirit. Yet, nothing happened until God released the Word. For God to repair the earth, or start His restoration of this earth, He spoke to it. He used words to create the universe. Once God spoke to the earth, the Holy Spirit went to work. The Holy Spirit's job is to manifest whatever the Word says. Nothing can stop this. As you can see, if something could stop the Word it would have done so at the beginning in Genesis 1. Nothing can stop God's Word from manifesting, when spoken as God would speak it. Here, God spoke and the darkness had to go. It had to disappear. Genesis 1:3 says, "*And God said, Let there be light: and there was light.*" In Hebrew, the phrase "*let there be light*" is translated, "Light be." God actually spoke directly to the thing He wanted to manifest; He commanded it to come forth—and it obeyed Him.

Did God spend any time talking about how dark it was? No. He did not deal with the darkness. He used His authority to deal only with light—the thing He wanted. Once it appeared, God continued to "say" and everything He said came to be. Finally, in Genesis 1:26, God said, *"Let us make man in our image, after our likeness...."* This means He was making man to operate as He does. It is normal for sons and daughters to take on the attributes of their parents. Talking like God should be viewed the same way. This perspective is critical to victorious living.

How does God operate? What is His modus operandi? He spoke things into existence; He changed and rearranged the earth, as well as natural things with words. This is confirmed again in Hebrews 11:3 which says, *"Through faith we understand that the worlds were framed by the word of God, so that the things which are seen were not made of things which do appear."* This means the material realm you see on earth is a product of the spiritual realm. Therefore, the earth is a copy of something in the spiritual realm. The physical image you see of yourself in the mirror is not the real you. It is just your body; if the real you left your body, your body would not continue to live. The only way material things exist is when they have a spiritual component. Nathan Stone, author of the book *Names of God,* puts it this way: "It is the Elohim Who by His mighty power creates the vast universe; Who says and it is done; Who brings into being what was not; by Whose Word the worlds were framed so that things which are seen were not made of things which do appear." [Hebrews 11:3]

Everything you see was made from something you cannot see with the natural eye. God followed this principle when He made the universe and when He made mankind. He not only made the worlds by something you cannot see, He also sustains the world by something you cannot see. This is clear in Hebrews, chapter 1.

God, who at sundry times and in diverse manners spake in time past unto the fathers by the prophets, hath in these last days spoken unto us by his Son, whom he hath appointed heir of all things, by whom also he made the worlds; who being the brightness of his glory, and the express image of his person, and upholding all things by the word of his power. [verses 1-3]

The Word created the world, and the Word sustains the world. Having established this method of operation, God made man to operate like Him and He turned the earth over to us to have dominion over it.

And God said, Let us make man in our image, after our likeness: and let them have dominion over the fish of the sea, and over the fowl of the air, and over the cattle, and over all the earth, and over every creeping thing that creepeth upon the earth. [Genesis 1:26]

In order for you to exercise that dominion, God gave you the ability to speak words. He did this because words have authority. Since you are made in His image, it follows that you should talk like God talks. If you say what God says, it will come to pass. And, if you say nothing, you will get nothing. If you say wrong things, wrong things will come to pass.

Too often people approach life as if they can just decide how they will operate. This is not God's way. You need to follow His instructions to know how to live victoriously. Proverbs 14:12 says, *"There is a way which seemeth right unto a man, but the end thereof are the ways of death."* Genesis, chapter 1, contains the outline of how God operated during the creation process so you have a pattern to follow. He then gave mankind (men and women) authority to rule over everything that is on the earth. God, therefore, was making mankind like Him. The way we were born-again confirms this legacy.

Being born again, not of corruptible seed, but of incorruptible, by the word of God, which liveth and abideth for ever. [1 Peter 1:23]

You were born by the Word of God and have undoubtedly heard the expression, "there's power in the Word"—meaning the Word of God. Are you living as if you believe this? John 1:1 says, *"In the beginning was the Word, and the Word was with God, and the Word was God."* Verse 14 in an expanded paraphrase says, "the Word took upon itself flesh." If you have God, you have the Word. If you have the Word, you have God. If you were born by the Word, you must have been born by God. We learn from Genesis 1:11-12 that every seed produces after its own kind. Therefore, you were born in God's class. You are called one of the children of God and absolutely must get this into your thinking. You are a child of God.

Therefore, you are to pattern yourself after Him. Jesus came as a "sample" son. As He began to operate in the earth, He began to pattern Himself after the Father. He said, "I do nothing except as I see my Father do it" [John 5:19 paraphrased]. In other words, He was learning it directly from the Father. The Father was teaching Him how to act and He was acting like the Father. Now, what does the Father do? The Father calls things that "be not" as though they were. When He saw darkness, He called it light.

You can follow this pattern if you change the way you see yourself. The right image on the inside will help you think right and therefore speak right. The Holy Ghost can teach you the right image.

But the Comforter, which is the Holy Ghost, whom the Father will send in my name, he shall teach you all things. [John 14:26]

Now we have received, not the spirit of the world, but the spirit which is of God; that we might know the things that are freely given to us of God. Which things also we speak, not in the words which man's wisdom teacheth, but which the Holy Ghost teacheth; comparing spiritual things with spiritual. [1 Corinthians 2:12-13]

God does not trust you to be taught by flesh because flesh does not know the whole story from God's point of view, but the Holy Ghost knows. He knows who you are and how you are supposed to act. Here is the design:

For ye see your calling, brethren, how that not many wise men after the flesh, not many mighty, not many noble, are called: but God hath chosen the foolish things of the world to confound the wise; and God hath chosen the weak things of the world to confound the things which are mighty; and base things of the world, and things which are despised, hath God chosen, yea, and things which are not, to bring to nought things that are.
[1 Corinthians 1:26-28]

God has chosen something that you cannot see to bring something that you can see to zero. God did not deal with what you could see. He did not say anything about how dark it was, how bad it was, or how terrible it was, and so forth. He just dealt with light—the thing He wanted. To do this He called light, and light brought darkness to zero. This is the pattern for living. God gave you the pattern first and then the promises.

God has given you these promises so that when you have a problem in your life, you do not need to go and tell everybody how bad it is. What you do is look in the Bible and get life—a promise through the Word of God. Focus on the desired result that is waiting in the unseen realm. This will cause the problem that *is* to become the problem that *was*. Now, it does not matter how bad your condition is. It was bad when God spoke to this earth, but what was bad became good when God's Word went forth. You may say, "Well, of course God can do that, but I'm just a human being." You are not just a human being. You are body, soul, and spirit. And God has given you His Word. His Word has the same power that it had when God first spoke it—it has not lost one ounce of power. What it did 6,000 years ago, it will do today. So all you have to do is take His Word and put it in your heart, let it come out of your mouth and the Word will bring your problem to zero.

You may ask, "What about the Holy Ghost?" At the creation, He was moving—brooding over the earth, but nothing happened. Why did nothing happen? Nothing happened because no one had spoken. Today, God's people are keeping quiet or saying the wrong things. For this to succeed, you need to speak God's Word. You may wonder, "Is the Holy Ghost still with us doing that?" The answer is "yes" according to 1 Corinthians 6:19... *"know ye not that your body is the temple of the Holy Ghost which is in you, which ye have of God, and ye are not your own?"*

This means the Holy Ghost is still moving. He is still here. He is still waiting on the Word. God is the same—He has not changed. He said, I am the Lord and I do not change. I have created you in my image and my likeness. The way I act, I want you to act that same way. You are to pattern your life after Jesus' life. Here is just one example of how He operated on earth as the Son of God when He walked by a fig tree.

And seeing a fig tree afar off having leaves, he came, if haply he might find any thing thereon: and when he came to it, he found nothing but leaves; for the time of figs was not yet. And Jesus answered and said unto it, No man eat fruit of thee hereafter for ever. And His disciples heard it. [Mark 11:13-14]

When this Word went forth, the spoken Word quickly manifested.

And in the morning, as they passed by, they saw the fig tree dried up from the roots. And Peter calling to remembrance saith unto him, Master, behold, the fig tree which thou cursedst is withered away. And Jesus answering saith unto them, Have faith in God. For verily I say unto you, That whosoever shall say unto this mountain, Be thou removed, and be thou cast into the sea; and shall not doubt in his heart, but shall believe that those things which he saith shall come to pass; he shall have whatsoever he saith. [Mark 11:20-23]

Natural or physical things are dominated or controlled by the more powerful things of the spirit. Therefore, your words are more than noise. Coming out of a believing heart, your words are spirit. They are designed to do things—they are designed to have authority on this earth. When you invoke this authority, God can act on it. In Mark 11:23, "say" or "saith" is mentioned three times. Believe is only mentioned once. This suggests it is easier "to believe" than to "say." In other words, the problem is saying. God says what He wants to manifest.

Look how He spoke to Gideon. Gideon was a man of low self-esteem and had a serious inferiority complex, hiding out from the Midianites, who were enemies of Israel. Then God spoke:

And the angel of the LORD appeared unto him, and said unto him, The LORD is with thee, thou mighty man of valour. And Gideon said unto him, Oh my LORD, if the LORD be with us, why then is all this befallen us? and where be all his miracles which our fathers told us of, saying, Did not the LORD bring us up from Egypt? but now the LORD hath forsaken us, and delivered us into the hands of the Midianites. And the LORD looked upon him, and said, Go in this thy might, and thou shalt save Israel from the hand of the Midianites: have not I sent thee? And he said unto him, O my Lord, wherewith shall I save Israel? behold, my family is poor in Manasseh, and I am the least in my father's house. And the LORD said unto him, Surely I will be with thee, and thou shalt smite the Midianites as one man. [Judges 6:12-16]

At the time of this visitation, Gideon looked like anything but a brave and mighty man. In fact, his conversation and his behavior were the exact opposite. God did not see Gideon the way Gideon saw himself. God did not speak about Gideon the way Gideon spoke about himself. Gideon, on the other hand, immediately responded out of his own image—my family is weak, I am the least in my dad's house, etc. But God had already designated him as a leader—a mighty man of valor. God has a plan and a destiny for your life, and He is going to call you how He wants you to be. It is important for you to line up your confession with how God sees you. Otherwise, you are actually disagreeing with God.

When God spoke about who Gideon was, He spoke out of faith. God is a faith God, and when we get born-again, the Bible says we receive the faith of God, so that we can operate like God. Therefore, this is how we are to live. *"The just shall live by faith"* [Romans 1:17]. God was not walking by what He saw, He was walking by what He wanted and desired in His heart. He clearly wants us to operate as He does because He made us in His image and likeness. He created man just like Him. You must decide in your mind to believe this and not back down from it, because sometimes religion can paint a different picture.

Mankind has a long, sad history of unbelief. In the Bible, by the time we read Isaiah 55:8-9, clearly man had fallen a long way from where God meant for him to be. It says, *"For my thoughts are not your thoughts, neither are your ways my ways, saith the* LORD. *For as the heavens are higher than the earth, so are my ways higher than your ways, and my thoughts than your thoughts."* In verse 11 it says, *"So shall my word be that goeth forth out of my mouth: it shall not return unto me void, but it shall accomplish that which I please, and it shall prosper in the thing whereto I sent it."*

Once you release God's Word, it will prosper. The Word will prosper. Not you, but the Word will prosper. The Word will accomplish what you want. But you have to first get His Word in your mouth and speak it from a believing heart and His Word will bring it to pass. This is so because there is enough power in God's Word to bring itself to pass. The Bible says in John 1:1, *"In the beginning was the Word, and the Word was with God, and the Word was God."* Verse 3 says, *"All things were made by him; and without him was not any thing made that was made."* Verse 14 says, *"And the Word was made flesh, and dwelt among us...."* Again, the expanded paraphrase version of verse 14 says, "The Word took upon itself flesh." So anytime you have the Word, you have God. Anytime you have God, you have the Word. Is there anything too hard for God? No. Is there anything too hard for the Word? No. With God, all things are possible. So if all things are possible with God, then all things are possible with His Word. When God's Word comes forth out of your mouth from a believing heart, it has the same power it had when God spoke in Genesis, chapter 1. This will work for whosoever believes. If you do not believe, it will not work for you.

What is God doing today? He is restoring all things. He is bringing us back to where we are supposed to be. That is why Jesus came. With His coming, the restoration process was moved to a whole new level. You have to begin connecting these spiritual truths to your life.

One day, when I was living in Tulsa attending Bible school we were about to have a meeting outside when a storm cloud came in rather suddenly, almost like it was a supernatural storm cloud. A gentleman named Ernie who was with me said, "Brother Bill, we better take this stuff inside. It's about to pour out here."

I said, "No it is not. Clouds, I am talking to you, in the name of Jesus. Sun, come back out." And it did not rain on our meeting. Here is the key. God's Word on your lips will enable you to walk in the same ability that God walked in, with that same Word. It is not you—it is God. It is His Word that He gave you permission to release. Not only does it have dominion power, but also creative power. Paul tells us to be imitators of God, as dear children (Ephesians 5:1). Therefore, we should talk like God talks.

According to this principle, you have to renew your mind and change your image. Living by the "power of the tongue" precept is a long way from what you have probably heard and believed most of your life. For instance, this teaching is a long way from the tentative songs of faith that people might have grown up singing or still sing in church—songs that include choruses such as, "Savior, Savior, hear my humble cry. While on others thou art calling, please don't pass me by." There is no teaching in the Bible that suggests the Savior might pass you by when you call upon Him. *"And it shall come to pass, that whosoever shall call on the name of the Lord shall be saved"* [Acts 2:21].

As a Believer, you may wonder, "What things do I apply this biblical teaching on the power of the tongue? Jesus spoke to a fig tree and a storm. What things should I speak to?" Since *"in the beginning was the Word, and the Word was with God, and the Word was God,"* you might ask, "What things do I apply truths about God to?" For instance, I spoke to my bills and my car and I got results. As God began to manifest Himself strong in these circumstances, I became a "professional" confessor; I began to make my living by speaking to things and circumstances. We can do this because God and Jesus did it. We can do this because God and Jesus did it. As joint-heirs with Christ [Romans 8:17], we are to follow these same examples. We have the authority to do so because in Genesis 1:26, God gave mankind "dominion." Dominion includes the right to issue edicts and directives—to take action. God used words to turn problems into triumphs. You must learn to speak and do likewise.

CHAPTER TWO

Words Have Creative Force

*Teach me, and I will
hold my tongue: and
cause me to understand
wherein I have erred.*

Job 6:24

When we plant a seed, we expect it to come up and produce after its kind. For instance, if we plant corn we expect corn to grow. Jesus said it is the same way with our words. He told a parable in Luke 8:5-8; 11-15 about a sower sowing seed. Jesus said:

> A sower went out to sow his seed: and as he sowed, some fell by the way side; and it was trodden down, and the fowls of the air devoured it. And some fell upon a rock; and as soon as it was sprung up, it withered away, because it lacked moisture. And some fell among thorns; and the thorns sprang up with it, and choked it. And other fell on good ground, and sprang up, and bare fruit an hundredfold...The seed is the word of God. Those by the way side are they that hear; then cometh the devil, and taketh away the word out of their hearts, lest they should believe and be saved. They on the rock are they, which, when they hear, receive the word with joy; and these have no root, which for a while believe, and in time of temptation fall away. And that which fell among thorns are they, which, when they have heard, go forth, and are choked with cares and riches and pleasures of this life, and bring no fruit to perfection. But that on the good ground are they, which in an honest and good heart, having heard the word, keep it, and bring forth fruit with patience.

Word as "seed" is an apt metaphor for this teaching on the power of the tongue. The dark side of this power is reflected in the story of the Tower of Babel.

> And the whole earth was of one language, and of one speech. And it came to pass, as they journeyed from the east, that they found a plain in the land of Shinar; and they dwelt there. And they said one to another, Go to, let us make brick, and burn them throughly. And they had brick for stone, and slime had they for morter. And they

said, Go to, let us build us a city and a tower, whose top may reach unto heaven; and let us make us a name, lest we be scattered abroad upon the face of the whole earth. And the LORD came down to see the city and the tower, which the children of men builded. And the LORD said, Behold, the people is one, and they have all one language; and this they begin to do: and now nothing will be restrained from them, which they have imagined to do. Go to, let us go down, and there confound their language, that they may not understand one another's speech. So the LORD scattered them abroad from thence upon the face of all the earth: and they left off to build the city. [Genesis 11:1-8]

The Tower of Babel was being built on words. It is true that brick and mortar were the materials, but words provided the inspiration to build—God said so. In fact, He was so concerned about the ability of words to bring this project to fruition that He confounded or confused the people's speech to interrupt the project. This is a classic example of how mankind's speech can initiate something that is not consistent with God's plan. Just think how much more you can get done if you speak according to God's plan versus contrary to His plan? Understanding the connection between your words and your life is critical. The Bible says:

Man shall not live by bread alone, but by every word that proceedeth out of the mouth of God. [Matthew 4:4]

This is why you must know God's Word. You must meditate on God's Word. Joshua 1:8 says: *"This book of the law shall not depart out of thy mouth; but thou shalt meditate therein day and night, that thou mayest observe to do according to all that is written therein: for then thou shalt make thy way prosperous, and then thou shalt have good success."* After meditating on God's Word, you must apply God's Word to every situation. Speaking God's Word puts "feet to your faith"—it builds you up in every part of your being.

Therefore, you must be careful about what you say. Words impact your spirit, soul, and body. The connection to the spirit is found in John 6:63, *"...the words that I speak unto you, they are spirit, and they are life,"* and Proverbs 26:22, *"The words of a tale-bearer are as wounds, and they go down into the innermost parts of the belly* (a person's spirit)." Proverbs 21:23 addresses the impact on the soul. It says, *"Whoso keepeth his mouth and his tongue keepeth his soul from troubles."* And then in Proverbs 16:24 it describes the impact on the body as follows: *"Pleasant words are as an honeycomb, sweet to the soul, and health to the bones."* Your tongue therefore, is the key to your life and destiny. *"A wholesome tongue is a tree of life: but perverseness therein is a breach in the spirit"* [Proverbs 15:4]. *"The mouth of a righteous man is a well* (source) *of life..."* [Proverbs 10:11]. *"He that keepeth his mouth keepeth his life..."* [Proverbs 13:3]. You either live by God's Word or by your own. There is no third option.

Thou art snared with the words of thy mouth, thou art taken with the words of thy mouth. [Proverbs 6:2]

The world system has trained you to use your tongue against yourself. For instance, you often hear people say, "I just tell it like it is." People even laud this personality trait. They say it is being "honest." Instead, you should tell it like you want it—not like it is. You also hear, "Give them a piece of your mind." If your mind is not renewed as described in Romans 12:2, you are giving them a "piece" of you that is not godly. Another popular expression is, "It blew my mind." That is exactly what the devil wants to do—blow your mind—to *"steal, kill, and destroy."* The devil uses your authority to trap you because he has none. What happens to your God-given dominion when this occurs? It is abdicated to the enemy. You are not using your authority either when: 1) You do not watch what you say, 2) You are not willing to speak right, and/or 3) You do not believe what you say. You are hung by the tongue. The enemy will even camp people around you so he can trap you with his words. Many of the chief rulers believed in Jesus but because of the Pharisees, they did not confess him. *"For they loved the praise of men more than the praise of God"* [John 12:43].

In Daniel, chapter 3, the king issued a death decree against those who would not bow and worship the image he created. But Daniel and his two companions made a positive confession. They did not discuss how hot it would be in the fiery furnace into which they were to be thrown or how evil the king was. They did not discuss his idol-worshipping decree that was causing them trouble. Instead they said, *"If it be so, our God whom we serve is able to deliver us from the burning fiery furnace, and he will deliver us out of thine hand, O king"* [verse 17].

When they were put in the furnace (that the king made seven times hotter, when they refused to bow), the king saw a fourth man in the furnace. When the king called for them to come out, all that were there *"...saw these men, upon whose bodies the fire had no power, nor was an hair of their head singed, neither were their coats changed, nor the smell of fire had passed on them"* [verse 27]. The word the Hebrew men had spoken manifested in the time of trouble! Now, either you believe this happened or you do not. Either you believe you have this kind of authority or you do not. Either you believe God is the same yesterday, today, and forever or you do not. It is this simple. If you believe it—then say it.

You need to understand so you can see how the enemy will turn up the heat to change your confession. This is when you must stand. This is when what is in you will come out of you. If the Word of God is in you, it will come out and bring to nought the thing that is and bring forth what is not. If God's Word is not in you, you are more prone to speak words confirming your problem thus helping the enemy wage war against you. For instance, you might say, "I'm never going to get out of debt" or "The doctor says there is no cure for this kind of cancer." Your mouth can be the ammunition that destroys you.

When you speak these things, the world says you are being "honest" and "straightforward." The world calls this "integrity." You might even feel wise or brave for being what many call "realistic." God's way is the way of wisdom and failing to speak forth His promises is not wisdom. Remember, two spiritual entities are waiting on your words to make sure they come to pass: angels and the enemy.

Bless the LORD, ye his angels, that excel in strength, that do his commandments, hearkening unto the voice of his word. [Psalm 103:20]

"Be sober, be vigilant; because your adversary the devil, as a roaring lion, walketh about, seeking whom he may devour." [1 Peter 5:8]

Therefore, there is no such thing as a "silent prayer." Our ignorance as God's people has kept us in bondage. When we repeat what our natural parents say, then surely we should repeat what our heavenly Father says.

You have said things that you thought might have been religiously correct or things that were socially acceptable against God, but were wrong. Sometimes people think because they do not say a four-letter word they are not cursing, but the Bible explains you can curse without saying a four-letter word. You can speak a curse over your life just as easily as Jesus cursed the unfruitful fig tree. Your mouth can be a weapon against you or a tool to help you.

The wicked is snared by the transgression of his lips: but the just shall come out of trouble. [Proverbs 12:13]

What does this scripture mean? It means your mouth will entrap you or deliver you. You might say, "Well, I can't watch every word!" Well, you had better because Jesus said in Matthew 12:36-

37, *"But I say unto you, That every idle word that men shall speak, they shall give account thereof in the day of judgment. For by thy words thou shalt be justified* (or made free), *and by thy words thou shalt be condemned."*

According to verse 34, the words you speak come out of your heart—which is a depository for words. It is a cycle: think, speak, deposit—speak, deposit, think. Whatever you think adds to the deposit and it becomes bigger. Whatever you speak again adds to the heart depository. So your thoughts and speech ultimately shape your life. This is why you must have God's Word in your depository and not your words. The things you speak are the things you think about or meditate on, and the words you receive from this kind of meditation go down into your heart.

If you are not mindful of the words on which you meditate, instead of being elevated above your situation, these thoughts will come up out of the heart depository in the form of words that do not line up with what God said about you—especially in times of trouble. When you speak on this lower level, you bring yourself right down to the level of your problems. The Israelites discovered this as noted in Numbers, chapter 13.

When the children of Israel came out of Egypt, they went into the wilderness and sent twelve spies to peruse the land of Canaan. Once they spied out that land, the twelve leaders, or authority figures, came back with a report. Ten of them came back with what the Bible calls an "evil report," which is a report that says something God did not say. God said the following about them going into the land. In fact, He said it centuries before their entry:

> Now the LORD had said unto Abram, Get thee out of thy country, and from thy kindred, and from thy father's house, unto a land that I will shew thee: and I will make of thee a great nation, and I will bless thee, and make thy

name great; and thou shalt be a blessing: and I will bless them that bless thee, and curse him that curseth thee: and in thee shall all families of the earth be blessed...And Abram took Sarai his wife, and Lot his brother's son, and all their substance that they had gathered, and the souls that they had gotten in Haran; and they went forth to go into the land of Canaan; and into the land of Canaan they came. And Abram passed through the land unto the place of Sichem, unto the plain of Moreh. And the Canaanite was then in the land. And the LORD appeared unto Abram, and said, Unto thy seed will I give this land: and there builded he an altar unto the LORD, who appeared unto him. [Genesis 12:1-7]

God did not say they were going to be slaughtered in Canaan or the inhabitants would eat them up. God did not say the buildings were so high that Israel could not take them or the cities. God said get in there; I am with you and I am going to give you victory. But what happened when the twelve spies came back?

And they went and came to Moses, and to Aaron, and to all the congregation of the children of Israel, unto the wilderness of Paran, to Kadesh; and brought back word unto them, and unto all the congregation, and shewed them the fruit of the land. And they told him, and said, We came unto the land whither thou sentest us, and surely it floweth with milk and honey; and this is the fruit of it. Nevertheless the people be strong that dwell in the land, and the cities are walled, and very great: and moreover we saw the children of Anak there. The Amalekites dwell in the land of the south: and the Hittites, and the Jebusites, and the Amorites, dwell in the mountains: and the Canaanites dwell by the sea, and by the coast of Jordan. [Numbers 13:26-29]

This evil report was given by ten of the spies. Only two of them—Joshua and Caleb—were confident in God's Word in the face of these facts. Caleb said, *"...Let us go up at once, and possess it; for we are well able to overcome it"* [verse 30]. This was a good report. But did it look like that in the natural realm? No, it did not. Caleb did not base his statement on what he saw or feared; he based it on what God had said. There was also past evidence of God's ability to deliver His people out of a tight spot. After all, He had just brought them out of Egypt against all odds.

> But the men that went up with him said, We be not able to go up against the people; for they are stronger than we. And they brought up an evil report of the land which they had searched unto the children of Israel, saying, The land, through which we have gone to search it, is a land that eateth up the inhabitants thereof; and all the people that we saw in it are men of a great stature. And there we saw the giants, the sons of Anak, which come of the giants: and we were in our own sight as grasshoppers, and so we were in their sight. And all the congregation lifted up their voice, and cried; and the people wept that night. And all the children of Israel murmured against Moses and against Aaron: and the whole congregation said unto them, Would God that we had died in the land of Egypt! or would God we had died in this wilderness! And wherefore hath the LORD brought us unto this land, to fall by the sword, that our wives and our children should be a prey? were it not better for us to return into Egypt? And they said one to another, Let us make a captain, and let us return into Egypt. [Numbers 13:31-33; 14:1-4]

Fear had control of the Israelites' hearts and tongues. Therefore, they gave voice to what they saw and felt. They confirmed the facts and not the truth. The fact was, the people in the land were strong and the cities were walled. However, the truth was that God promised to give them the land.

In the face of this "evil report," God still had a voice.

> And Joshua the son of Nun, and Caleb the son of Jephunneh, which were of them that searched the land, rent their clothes: And they spake unto all the company of the children of Israel, saying, The land, which we passed through to search it, is an exceeding good land. If the LORD delight in us, then he will bring us into this land, and give it us; a land which floweth with milk and honey. Only rebel not ye against the LORD, neither fear ye the people of the land; for they are bread for us: their defence is departed from them, and the LORD is with us: fear them not. [Numbers 14:6-9]

Their unbelief and rebellion so angered the Lord that He was provoked to great wrath and threatened to smite them with pestilence, to disinherit them, and to form a new nation. Fortunately, Moses interceded with a heartfelt plea to the Lord. *"And the Lord said, I have pardoned according to thy word"* [verse 20]. However, there was a price to pay for the words the ten spies had spoken:

> And the LORD spake unto Moses and unto Aaron, saying, How long shall I bear with this evil congregation, which murmur against me? I have heard the murmurings of the children of Israel, which they murmur against me. Say unto them, As truly as I live, saith the LORD, as ye have spoken in mine ears, so will I do to you: Your carcases shall fall in this wilderness; and all that were numbered of you, according to your whole number, from twenty years old and upward, which have murmured against me, doubtless ye shall not come into the land, concerning which I

sware to make you dwell therein, save Caleb the son of Jephunneh, and Joshua the son of Nun. [verses 26-30]

The impact of words is not to be taken lightly. Saying what God says might subject you to ridicule—even by church people—or even the threat of death as we see with Joshua and Caleb. You are not going to be popular for speaking what God wants you to say because the whole world system is against God. Satan is behind that system and he is deceiving people. As we often see, his way leads to death. The outcome for the ten spies who gave the evil report was consistent with what they said:

And the men, which Moses sent to search the land, who returned, and made all the congregation to murmur against him, by bringing up a slander upon the land, even those men that did bring up the evil report upon the land, died by the plague before the LORD. [verses 36-37]

Not only did they die, but their words resulted in a whole generation of people dying in the wilderness after wandering there for forty years, never entering the Promised Land [verses 33-35]. There is a good lesson in this passage about following the majority. Do not follow someone because they are in the majority; this applies to all areas of life—work, politics, family, etc. The majority might be bringing up a slanderous report and depending upon their position, they could put a slander report on an entire city. The Bible says with a man's tongue he can bring a city to ruin, and with a man's tongue, he can build it back up. [See Proverbs 11:11]

Abraham grasped the impact of words on his life as he waited for God's promise to manifest. He knew in order to change his life he had to change his confession—how he described himself. He could no longer call himself impotent. Such a confession was contrary to God's promise. In the face of natural law (his body was old and past the years in which men can sire children), Abraham had to cite spiritual law (which was God's promise that He would make of him a great nation through a child of his own body).

How does this process translate into your life? The same way it did in Abraham's life. You can no longer call yourself sick or broke saying, "I can't afford that." These are words we have been trained by the world system to speak, but they are absolutely out of line with God's Word and we cannot say these things anymore.

God is trying to bring us over into a place where we can operate and be a laborer with Him to build His Kingdom. We cannot "tell it like it is." We have to tell it like we want it. So Abraham had to call things that be not as though they were. He had to call what he wanted.

Maybe your doctor gave you an evil report, like the evil report when they came out of Canaan. Nevertheless, Joshua and Caleb gave a good report. They said, *"We are well able,"* and they said this against all odds. To the natural eyes it did not look like they were well able, but they were not calling things they saw. They were calling things they wanted. And you can do this, too, without being a hypocrite. Unfortunately, the Church has not taught us that.

Therefore, the Church, for the most part, has been in the wilderness. We have been saved, but we have not been living the fullness of life. We are going to have to declare war on those things. We are going to have to say, "Wait a minute! Let God be true and every man be a liar." We have to say what God said and disregard those who do not like it. I do not care if it harelips the devil. I am going to say what God says, *"By His stripes I am healed."* If you do not do this, the enemy will try to tempt you, to intimidate you into making you think you are lying. Ask the devil this, "Devil, how can I lie saying what God said?"

CHAPTER THREE

What Did Jesus Say?

I said, I will take heed to my ways, that I sin not with my tongue: I will keep my mouth with a bridle, while the wicked is before me.

Psalm 39:1

Jesus set an excellent example for us on how to use our tongue for victorious living. In Mark 4:35-38, it says, *"And the same day, when the even was come, he saith unto them, Let us pass over unto the other side. And when they had sent away the multitude, they took him even as he was in the ship. And there were also with him other little ships. And there arose a great storm of wind, and the waves beat into the ship, so that it was now full. And he was in the hinder part of the ship, asleep on a pillow: and they awake him, and say unto him, Master, carest thou not that we perish?"*

Where do you think this question came from? It did not come from God. It came from the circumstances they saw. Remember God's pattern He set at creation. When He saw darkness, He called it light—He did not deal with the darkness.

So when Jesus was in that storm, what did He do?

He arose, and rebuked the wind, and said unto the sea, Peace, be still. And the wind ceased, and there was a great calm. And he said unto them, Why are ye so fearful? how is it that ye have no faith? And they feared exceedingly, and said one to another, What manner of man is this, that even the wind and the sea obey him? [Mark 4:39-41]

A man once told me that in Greek, the word *beat*, describing the nature of the storm, means "waves coming over and thrusting down" or "to throw one's self up on, rush upon: waves rushing into a ship." In other words, a situation put pressure on the disciples' minds. The devil puts pressure on your mind to say what he wants you to say.

For instance, when the finances look bad or the marriage looks bad, the enemy pressures you to say what he wants you to say. Why? Because he is waiting to carry out the words you speak; he definitely wants it to be a negative. We must release the Word of

God and the Word will deal with the problem, defeating the devil's plans. What Jesus did with that storm was teach us that we can speak to the natural world and it will obey us.

If you have a situation in your life, do not deal with the situation by talking about it. You have to completely trust God and deal only with His promises. You must call things that be not as though they were. When the Word of the promise comes alive, the Word deals with the problem. The Word can deal with the problem much better than you can deal with it. It can straighten out your whole situation. It is hard to say, "I believe everything is going to be alright," when it looks as if all pandemonium has broken loose. It is hard to say it because we have been trained in the "sense realm." We have been trained that it is logical to say what we see. *"They that observe lying vanities forsake their own mercy"* [Jonah 2:8]. You have got to train your senses to bow to your spirit.

Your body is not your boss. It works for you. You have to stop and realize even though a situation looks bad, it is not true when it does not line up with the Word of God. It may be a fact, but it is not true. What you have to do is focus on the truth. Meditate on the truth. Confess the truth. Believe the truth, and the truth will come alive, and when the truth comes alive, it will deal with the problem. God's Word is truth and if you have God's Word, you have God. He can deal with the problem—even while you are asleep.

Many people watch the news on television right before going to sleep at night. They file bad news in their minds and then go to bed. They might even dream about it and wake up the next morning with it on their minds. This is a form of meditation, except it is meditating on bad news that generates negative thoughts. The same meditation can be done on God's Word that generates encouraging thoughts, positive thoughts, and truthful thoughts that build your faith.

Meditation involves repetition. Here is an example of how it can work. Evangelist R. W. Schambach told a story about an incident that happened during his childhood when he was unsaved. He said he and some of the other boys were in class but they did not feel like having school. So one of them told the teacher, "You know you don't look too well today." And she said, "Oh go back and sit down." They waited another 15 or 20 minutes, and another student went up and said, "Teacher, you don't look too good today." She said, "Would you go back, sit down, and do the work that I have assigned you to do?" He went back and sat down. After about a half-hour the teacher sent the students out to do something, and another boy passed by and said, "Teacher, are you all right?" And she said, "Why do you ask?" The boy said, "You don't look too well today."

They worked that teacher over about four times, and at that point she said she was dismissing the class because she did not feel well and she needed to go home. My point is that the devil tries to work you over, and he sends all kinds of messengers to confirm a negative word: "You're sick; You're never gonna be able to get out of debt; Your marriage can't be fixed; Your child won't ever get off drugs; You're going to get laid off; or, There is no cure for cancer." In these times, remember God's pattern. Say what He said about your situation—regardless of how things appear. Simon Peter took God at His Word and was blessed.

> Now when he had left speaking, he said unto Simon, Launch out into the deep, and let down your nets for a draught. And Simon answering said unto him, Master, we have toiled all the night, and have taken nothing: nevertheless at thy word I will let down the net. And when they had this done, they inclosed a great multitude of fishes: and their net brake. And they beckoned unto their partners, which were in the other ship, that they should come and help them. And they came, and filled both the ships, so that they began to sink. [Luke 5:4-7]

Peter fished for a living and he was a "pro." But even "pros" have off-days when they have to work hard to stay a pro. When Peter received Jesus' Words and acted on them, he received an abundance that his "toiling" did not bring. Many people today work very hard and get very little. What made the difference in Simon's life? The Word. The first Word for him was that he was a seed of Abraham and God promised to bless Abraham's seed so that everything they laid their hands on would be blessed. In the passage above, Simon's boat represented the seed. Jesus used Simon's boat to bless him. But the first seed Simon had to get was the Word of God—not just part of it. The most critical part of the Word for him was the part that prospered his soul. *"The law of the LORD is perfect, converting the soul..."* [Psalm 19:7]. In 3 John 2, it says, *"Beloved, I wish above all things that thou mayest prosper and be in health, even as thy soul prospereth."* Therefore, the Word is the most important seed we can sow. It is this process that renews our minds and changes our thinking, which changes our speech.

I can personally attest to this in my own life. I started my ministry in the basement of a friend's home, Sister Beverly's, in a Chicago suburb. There was my wife, my son, Sister Beverly, and I—us four and no more. But the Word went out and people came to hear it. We then moved to a Quality Inn for our meetings, and one day a lawyer attending our services said to me, "I heard you talked to some bills. I am so deep in debt. Can you come down to my office and talk to my bills?" So I went down to his office and he closed the door. He had a stack of bills on his desk. I looked at these debt statements and said, "Bills, we're talking to you in Jesus' Name." I said, "Shut up," because bills will talk back to you. I then proceeded with my directive in the Name of Jesus. After a while, the attorney reported his bills were paid off and his finances were restored to the point that he became a very wealthy person.

It takes faith to talk like God talks. Jesus says, *"...If ye had faith as a grain of mustard seed, ye might say unto this sycamine tree, Be thou plucked up by the root, and be thou planted in the sea; and it should obey you"* [Luke 17:6]. Jesus made this statement while teaching on forgiveness. There may be people in your life who have hurt you and you need to forgive them. Perhaps you have been saying, "I just can't forgive them." God's way of removing this obstacle is to say what you desire, not what you see or feel. The more you say you cannot forgive, the bigger this mountain gets because your words are connected to your life. But Jesus says your faith does not have to be big to overcome this stronghold. This problem will obey your words spoken in faith. Anything God says in His Word that you want, you are going to have to get by faith, not by feelings. Faith comes through the Word.

CHAPTER FOUR

Taking Jesus Public/
Closet Christians

*My tongue is
the pen of a
ready writer.*

Psalm 45:1

When we were in Tulsa and I was attending Bible school full-time, my wife Veronica was looking for a job. Before our ministry started, we had both worked for IBM, so she was seeking a job in computers. She went around to some of the employment agencies and they told her no one was hiring and companies were laying off hundreds of people. Call it an evil report. When she came back home, we discussed the situation and I said, "Wait a minute. We are not going to let the circumstances govern us." So here is what she did. She got a 3x5 index card and we designed her perfect job. Now, our thinking at this point was a long way from the sentiments expressed in a song we used to sing containing the refrain "Savior do not pass me by." You have to guard your heart. If you keep hearing that message, you will start believing that He will pass you by and the words you speak may be consistent with that outcome—God may answer your prayer or He may just pass you by. God said, call on Me and I will answer you, every time.

My wife and I had no thoughts of the Savior passing us by. So, she wrote down everything she wanted in this job—computer work, a ten-minute ride from the house, a nice office, and a certain salary. She wanted a car with the job, so we wrote that down, too. She got the scriptures that agreed with what she desired and we came into agreement for this job.

Where did she put the scriptures? The Bible says to keep the Word of God before your eyes [Proverbs 4:21]. She put them all over the house. I would go look out a window and a card with a scripture written on it was there. Everywhere I looked, the scriptures were there—in the bedroom, in the kitchen, even in the bathroom. I would open the refrigerator and see a card with "I am redeemed from the curse" written on it. At this point, we were not focusing on the problem anymore. We had turned our focus away from the problem and put our focus on the answer because we understood the answer, God's Word, would deliver us from the problem.

God told Joshua to attend to His (God's) Words. He told him this because only God's Word can reverse the curse Adam loosed on the earth. God said, *"This book of the law shall not depart out of thy* (Joshua's) *mouth; but thou shalt meditate therein day and night, that thou mayest observe to do according to all that is written therein: for then thou shalt make thy way prosperous, and then thou shalt have good success"* [Joshua 1:8]. I have this scripture in me and I discovered God does not make my way prosperous. Of course, He is behind it, but it is up to me to take actions to make my way prosperous. It is up to me to have good success, and it starts with meditating on God's Word day and night. I needed to give the Word first place in my life if I was going to have prosperity in the middle of a situation where I did not know how I was going to prosper.

With this in mind, my wife kept the answer before her. She was talking about things not visible in the natural realm (her new job via God's biblical promises) to bring to zero things visible in the natural realm (unemployment). Having the scriptures all over the house kept the promise before her and kept her from talking about the problem. When you are focused or preoccupied with God's Word and not the problem, you will be tested by the enemy. One day, a gentleman came by the house while my wife was on the front lawn and he said, "Hey, Sister Veronica, is Bill in? She said, "Yes. He is in the house." He asked, "Do you have your job yet?" She said, "I sure do." He said, "Where is it?" She said, "I don't know, but I got it." Meditating on God's Word prepares you for moments like this. Otherwise, your flesh will give the opposite response.

It takes courage to speak God's promise. Unfortunately, some people are not willing to do this. They will read about the promise and even quote it over someone else's trouble. When they hear it in church, they say "Amen" and "Hallelujah" at the appropriate times. But when pressure comes on them, too often they say what the world system says. For example, this is a possible conversation:

"Do you have your job yet?" Answer: "No, the employment agency hasn't found me anything yet. It's been a while and it doesn't look too good because of the economy and all." Reply: "Well, good luck." My wife held fast to her profession of faith.

Shortly after the incident with the gentleman visitor, my wife got a call. When she got off the telephone, she said, "Well, they (the employment agency) want to see me." I said, "Why?" She said, "They think they have something for me." So she went down for an interview, came home, and said, "Here is the report. Get the card out." So I got out the 3x5 index card and went down the list. I said, "Is it in computers?" She said, "Yes." We checked that off the list. "How about ten minutes from the house?" She said, "Yes, it's about nine and a half." I checked that off. "Well, how about the money?" She said, "They are paying me $5,000 more than what we put on the card." I said, "How about an automobile?" She said, "They told me to pick out a new Buick." This is an example of a person making her way prosperous by following God's pattern.

God has already prospered you, but He needs your participation to make it manifest. Meanwhile, the enemy will try to come against you and con you out of what belongs to you. He will give you several reasons why you are not supposed to get what God has promised you. Biblical meditation prepares you for these times, and if you follow God's pattern you will prevail, and all Glory be to God!

This process involves taking Jesus public. You cannot hide in your house when your faith is tested. You must take the Word public, not in an arrogant offensive manner just to show off, but in a Christ-confident manner, especially when you are challenged. Too many Christians stay in the closet at these moments—even when it comes time to pray over their food in a public place. You do not have to shout to the whole restaurant, but the time to stop denying God is now—even in these so-called "small matters."

Since you do not know who is preparing the food, it is wise to first ask God's blessing over it. If you are out with friends, just say "Excuse me, I am going to pray over this food right now." I understand on one occasion Smith Wigglesworth, a famous English minister in the early 1900s, was in a restaurant with his friends and after their food was served he said, "Are you ready to pray?" At that point, he reportedly took his glass, stood up, and tapped a piece of silverware against it to call everyone in the restaurant to attention. He then said, "All right you need to pray," and he prayed aloud for all within earshot. Not everyone is led to do what Wigglesworth did, but all Believers should be led to work the spiritual laws associated with speaking God's Word—even in public. The day for closet Christians is over—God is watching you.

What the enemy will do is place people around you—right at the lunch table—to test your resolve. Maybe they are some important people, your boss or clients, and you are wondering whether you should bow your head. Because of the thoughts running through your mind at this point, this situation is more than just a religious ritual now. It is a battle between you and the enemy. But Jesus said in Luke 12:8-9,

> Whosoever shall confess Me before men, him shall the Son of man also confess before the angels of God: but he that denieth Me before men shall be denied before the angels of God.

The point is this: learn to identify these situations when the enemy tries to keep you from operating in the principle of confessing God before men. Remember, you are not trying to impress people; you are trying to invoke spiritual laws. Some of you bless your food under these circumstances so quickly your fellow diners do not even know what you did. They might even think you were just looking down at your food. Others make such a show of it that they turn people off to the Gospel. But you can simply say, "Excuse me for a moment." Then bow your head and say your prayer, or include others at your table, as you feel led to do by the Holy Spirit. This might seem like a little thing, but if this is awkward for you, what will you do in other situations when it is time to confess Christ?

When I backed away from my stalled car that cold winter day to speak to it, I looked to see if anybody was looking—I do not look anymore. Remember what Peter said to Jesus before Jesus was betrayed and crucified, when everything was nice and quiet? He basically told Jesus he would be with Him no matter what. But when the pressure came on Peter, he not only denied him, but he denied him to the point of swearing an oath. Nevertheless, this same Peter was the first pastor of the first church because of his boldness.

At first, you will be a little shy taking these steps of faith in front of people; I was like that. I remember after I first got saved, and at the time, I was driving a red Corvette (that the devil later stole) and I had my Bible on the seat. I happened to be driving by some of my friends and they beckoned to me. As I pulled over to the side of the road to chat, I took the Bible and put it under the seat. But, thank God, we go from faith to faith. In other words, we go through different phases wherein God possesses us more and more, and He is patient. He has more time than we do. As you take this journey, your fear of speaking up will diminish.

Jesus was successful because He always did what the Father said to do. He just did it no matter the situation and regardless of what people said about Him.

The disciple is not above his master, nor the servant above his lord. It is enough for the disciple that he be as his master, and the servant as his lord. If they have called the master of the house Beelzebub, how much more shall they call them of his household? Fear them not therefore: for there is nothing covered, that shall not be revealed; and hid, that shall not be known. What I tell you in darkness, that speak ye in light: and what ye hear in the ear, that preach ye upon the housetops. [Matthew 10:24-27]

They called Jesus the devil. Some called Him the prince of devils. So, if they called Him the devil, you can expect to be called the same for following His example. The Bible says "all that will live godly in Christ Jesus shall suffer persecution" [2 Timothy 3:12]. Now, understand, the criterion is you live godly. All who live worldly may not suffer any persecution. The devil does not want you to take Jesus public or to have any supernatural help. He wants to keep your confession down—to keep you from speaking the things God would have you speak. This is acceptable in many places today, even in the religious community. Sometimes pressure comes from all sides, but be encouraged by the victories of those who have gone before us.

In Daniel, chapter 3, (as I referenced earlier) there were three Hebrew men (Shadrach, Meshach, and Abed-nego) facing a challenge. They were enslaved in Babylon and the world system was trying to make them bow down and worship a golden image King Nebuchadnezzar had built. The choice was to bow or burn in a fiery furnace. But these three Hebrews refused to bow even though *"...all the people, the nations, and the languages, fell down and worshipped the golden image..."* [Daniel 3:7]. Nebuchadnezzar was incensed and threatened them again with the fiery furnace, asking:

Who is that God that shall deliver you out of my hands? Shadrach, Meshach, and Abed-nego, answered and said to the king, O Nebuchadnezzar, we are not careful to answer thee in this matter. If it be so, our God whom we serve is able to deliver us from the burning fiery furnace, and he will deliver us out of thine hand, O king. But if not, be it known unto thee, O king, that we will not serve thy gods, nor worship the golden image which thou hast set up. [Daniel 3:15-18]

This is taking Jesus public before an important person; taking Him public despite what the majority does—taking Him public in the face of death. You know the Lord is able. We all know the Lord is able, but will He be able for you? I promise you He will. The Bible says in Hebrews 2:18 that Jesus is able to *"succour"* us. *Succour* means "come to your aid." I do not know about you, but I am on aid. Jesus is holding me up like He upheld the Hebrew young men. When the king had them thrown into the furnace, even the men who threw them in were burned up because the fire was so hot. But when the king looked into the fire, he was astonished and asked his counselors, *"...Did not we cast three men bound into the midst of the fire? They answered and said unto the king, True, O king. He answered and said, Lo, I see four men loose, walking in the midst of the fire, and they have no hurt; and the form of the fourth is like the Son of God"* [Daniel 3:24-25]. Then the king addressed Shadrach, Meshach, and Abed-nego as *"ye servants of the most high God"* and called them to come out of the furnace. *"Nor was an hair of their head singed, neither were their coats changed, nor the smell of fire had passed on them"* [Daniel 3:27]. That verse also says the *"...princes, governors, and captains, and the king's counsellors"* gathered together and saw these men after their ordeal. They took Jesus public and He then took them public.

When we moved from Lake and Pulaski street on the West Side of Chicago to Forest Park, Illinois, some of the members did not want to go, as they felt called to stay. So we came with about 15 members. After the move, I began looking at the members and looking at the rent that was due on the first of the month. I began to wonder how we were going to meet the church expenses. Then

God told me a couple of things: 1) People are not my source, and 2) He could meet my needs by many or by few [1 Samuel 14:6]. At this point, I had two choices—believe God or believe what I saw in the natural realm.

The Hebrews went through this when they came out of Egypt. They had been making bricks and building the world system. That system fed and clothed them, but they were still slaves. So God sent a deliverer. He sent Moses who led the people out, through the Red Sea and into the wilderness. When they got hungry or had a need, their mindset automatically converted back to Egypt and the way their needs were met when they were in bondage. So they were looking for a Dominick's, a Safeway, or a Piggly Wiggly. They were looking for something that made sense to the natural mind. But God took them out of Egypt and brought them into a place where there was nothing. He did this on purpose to teach them His way.

God will lead you into a task bigger than what you can do in your own natural ability. At this point, you are going to have to start calling things that be not as though they were. This is where God had brought our church when we moved to Forest Park. So, what did we start saying? We said, "Thank You, Lord, we have three services full on Sunday mornings. People are lined up down the sidewalk, waiting to get into the next service."

My wife and I were praying this every week. Even though we only had 15 people in the congregation, we continued to declare it week after week. We were calling things that be not as though they were, and the next thing we knew the place started filling up. We went to two services and they filled up. Then three services and they filled up. We put chairs in the lobby and out in the hall; chairs were everywhere. People were packed in like "sardines in a can" trying to hear the Word of God.

This only happened because the Word of God was at work. It was not about me. It is always about God's Kingdom being built as He ordained. God promised me that He would not let me be ashamed. He promised me that whatever I did would prosper. He promised me that He would be with me. With three services full and overflowing, people were standing outside waiting to get in. I even had one of the officials with the Village of Forest Park come by to see me one weekday. He said, "Reverend, what are you doing here? People are lined up all down the street. What is going on in here?" I said, "The Word is going forth." When you confess the Word, it first changes your image, and then it changes your circumstances. This is God's way. It is the first order of business. Once your image is changed, taking Jesus public then becomes your modus operandi.

CHAPTER FIVE

Heart Conditions

*The tongue of the just is
as choice silver.*

Proverbs 10:20

"I don't believe. I don't think. I can't." So often, our conversation is peppered with these words. This is driven by how we see ourselves as opposed to how God sees us. Look at Moses in Exodus, chapter 4. When God called him to set Israel free, Moses said, I can't talk. God asked Moses, who made your mouth? God did not need Moses to work out at the health club for Moses to do what He wanted him to do. He just needed his mouth. God needs your mouth. Moses went down to Egypt and every time he declared something, God made it happen. Life experiences drive this "I can't" thinking and shapes our self-images. Consequently, many people have an image problem as Moses did at first. Gideon (another Old Testament Israelite) had an image problem, too, but God quickly fixed it. In Gideon's day the "...*children of Israel did evil in the sight of the* LORD: *and the* LORD *delivered them into the hand of Midian seven years*" [Judges 6:1]. Eventually, the Israelites "...*cried unto the* LORD *because of the Midianites*" [verse 7].

And there came an angel of the LORD, and sat under an oak which was in Ophrah, that pertained unto Joash the Abiezrite: and his son Gideon threshed wheat by the winepress, to hide it from the Midianites. And the angel of the LORD appeared unto him, and said unto him, The LORD is with thee, thou mighty man of valour. And Gideon said unto him, Oh my Lord, if the LORD be with us, why then is all this befallen us? and where be all his miracles which our fathers told us of, saying, Did not the LORD bring us up from Egypt? but now the LORD hath forsaken us, and delivered us into the hands of the Midianites. And the LORD looked upon him, and said, Go in this thy might, and thou shalt save Israel from the hand of the Midianites: have not I sent thee? And he said unto him, Oh my Lord, wherewith shall I save Israel? behold, my family is poor in Manasseh, and I am the least in my father's house. And the LORD said unto him, Surely I will be with thee, and thou shalt smite the Midianites as one man. [verses 11-16]

In summary, the Israelites sinned. They eventually figured out that they should pray (say) to God. God heard them and took action to deliver them. He chose Gideon as His instrument, but first God had to perform some heart surgery on Gideon. While Gideon was acting like anything but a valiant and brave man, God called him "a mighty man of valour." That is because God knew the end from the beginning. Furthermore, God knew that the truth would make Gideon free. First, He had to get Gideon up to speed. Gideon was operating on a lie spawned by the enemy; he had a grasshopper mentality. As a result, Gideon responded he could not deliver Israel because of his family background and financial situation. In other words, Gideon said something God did not say. God countered by saying He would be with Gideon. And He was. God took Gideon's army of 32,000 men and pared it down to 300. He sent them into victorious battle with only trumpets and a battle cry, "...the sword of the LORD, and of Gideon" [Judges 7:18]. God changed Gideon's self-image (or heart). The new image changed his speech. The right speech changed Israel's situation.

The words we use to describe ourselves come from a reservoir deep within us. This reservoir in biblical terms is called the "heart." Jesus addressed this in very direct terms.

> O generation of vipers, how can ye, being evil, speak good things? for out of the abundance of the heart the mouth speaketh. A good man out of the good treasure of the heart bringeth forth good things: and an evil man out of the evil treasure bringeth forth evil things. But I say unto you, That every idle word that men shall speak, they shall give account thereof in the day of judgment. For by thy words thou shalt be justified, and by thy words thou shalt be condemned. [Matthew 12:34-37]

The "heart" Jesus is referring to in this passage is not the organ that pumps blood throughout the body. He is talking about the "spirit man." The heart is a container, a bucket that holds things. Your heart or spirit man is the same way. It is the real you. It holds spiritual things and the spiritual things it holds are words. Whatever words are in there, in abundance, will come out of your mouth. These words may not come out when you're sitting in church and everything is cool, the music is good, and everybody around you loves Jesus. It's when you go out into the world, when things happen, and pressure comes against you, that's when the real you will manifest in the form of speech. The trigger may be something a co-worker or your spouse says that prompts a negative response from you.

You might even have made a commitment that you will not say certain things anymore—regardless of the circumstance. Look at Peter. He thought he had it made. He told the Lord he would never forsake him, but everything was cool when he said this. Once things in the world put pressure on him, Peter suddenly said he did not know Jesus. He spoke this out of the abundance or "treasure" of his heart.

The "treasure of the heart" refers to a deposit. So, a man out of the deposit of his heart can bring forth good things or evil things, depending upon what is in him. "Bring forth" means sometime in the future. Therefore, you must check your heart, because whatever is in it is going to be your future. If you want your future to stay the same, just keep saying what you have been saying. If you want your future to change, you need to say something different because what you sow is what you are going to reap. Abraham had to learn to say something different. God even changed his name from Abram to Abraham to reflect what was going to be brought forth. Abraham means "father of a multitude." So every time someone called Abraham by his new name, they were affirming God's promise to give him and Sarah a son.

How does this apply to your life? Depending on your situation, it may mean you cannot call yourself sick anymore. Call yourself healed by His stripes [Isaiah 53:5]. You cannot call yourself broke anymore; instead declare, *"...My God shall supply all my needs according to his riches in glory by Christ Jesus"* [Philippians 4:19]. When I began to meditate on this, I compared it to my experience as a pilot. In flying an airplane, one of the things you do is get instructions from the controller. They might say "Bravo 66, turn right. Heading 360, maintain 3000." What do you do? You have to say what they said. "Roger. Bravo 66 turning right, heading 360, maintaining 3000." You have to say exactly what the controller said and everything will be all right. God knows how to direct you home. All you have to do is say what He said and follow His instructions.

Many words have come out of the "deposits" of many people, and made there way into our popular culture and into our vocabularies and are now socially acceptable in a lot of circles. For instance, "You blew my mind" is a common expression. Could this be an "idle word?" I am not advocating rigid legalism. I am advocating awareness. The Bible makes it clear that God wants to tighten up our speech to protect us from ourselves and from the enemy. Discipline starts with small things, as it should with our speech.

Learning to harness the power of the tongue is essential to victorious living. Always remember, your body is not your boss. It is a temporary house—an outer covering or suit for your spirit; it has no investment in eternity. Paul talks about the war between the flesh and the spirit. He said:

> For the good that I would I do not: but the evil which I would not, that I do. Now if I do that I would not, it is no more I that do it, but sin that dwelleth in me. I find then a law, that, when I would do good, evil is present with

me. For I delight in the law of God after the inward man.
[Romans 7:19-22]

The "inward man" is your spirit—the real you. When you die,
your body goes back to the dust and decomposes. But the real you
lives forever. For those who do not know God, the real you or person goes to a holding cell in Hades until the Great White Throne
Judgment. Those who have accepted Jesus as Lord and Savior go
to Paradise. Our focus then should be on the *"hidden man of the
heart"* and not on *"adorning"* the outer man as is written in 1 Peter
3:1-4.

Your "heart" is your core or center. When you speak words and
say things, they not only come from your mouth, but they go down
into your heart and into the spirit man. The spirit man or heart
holds these words, and external factors prompt them to come out
again. This process births your belief system. Therefore, nothing
you say is to be taken lightly because *"every idle word that* (you)
shall speak, (you) *shall give account thereof in the day of judgment"*
[Matthew 12:36]. Clearly, words are to be measured. They are to
be something over which you should exercise stewardship. Make
sure you say what you want to come to pass *"for by your words
you will be justified, and by your words you will be condemned"*
[Matthew 12:37 NASB]. You shall be acquitted or set free by your
words, or you will be put in bondage by your own words.

What is the enemy's strategy? His strategy is to control your
words; to use your own authority to put you in bondage. He wants
to stop you by using your speech. But death and life are not in the
power of the devil. It is in your power. The enemy has to use your
power to get to you. If you believe good things come from God,
then say so; God watches over His Word to perform it. But, if you
say things against God, have them in your heart, believe them, and
speak them, the devil is watching over those words and once you
release them, he has license to try to bring them to pass. Therefore,

you have to guard your heart and bridle your own tongue. We cannot say things that we do not want to happen.

The ten Israelite spies who gave the evil report after spying out Canaan saw the same things Joshua and Caleb saw. Yet they gave a negative report. People do not see with their eyes—they see through them. The content of the heart shapes a person's worldview and the enemy comes to blind the mind, and out of this darkness comes words of despair.

Even the world system has speech control protocols. As people ascend the corporate ladder, their words and their conversation changes and it becomes more important because they understand the impact of what they say. If they can say one wrong thing, it could cause trouble for the whole corporation. This is simply one of many responsibilities that accompany increased authority. As your role in God's Kingdom advances, you have to watch your heart deposits; you have to dispense it with temperance and wisdom. The passage in Matthew 12:34 says your future is inside of you. At this very moment, tomorrow is inside of you and somebody put it there. Deposits are made daily and this is why the Bible says to be careful what you hear. You might hear God does not heal everybody, and if this is deposited in your heart, this is what you will believe. This is what you will speak and that is what you will experience or receive.

This teaching is not designed to bind you. It is designed to help you identify where you are in the process of living—to raise your understanding and awareness about the power of words and how they shape you. *"Faith cometh by hearing, and hearing by the word of God"* [Romans 10:17], but other belief systems can also come by hearing. To correct this, you first need "heart surgery" and then speech replacement therapy. For example:

Instead of saying: I can't afford that.
Say: With God, all things are possible.
Instead of saying: I'm sick.
Say: By His stripes, I am healed.
Instead of saying: I'm tired.
Say: The joy of the Lord is my strength.
Instead of saying: I don't know how to do that.
Say: God teaches me to prosper.
Instead of saying: I'm lonely.
Say: God said He'll never leave me nor forsake me.
Instead of saying: I'm barren.
Say: Many are the afflictions of the righteous, but
God will deliver me out of them all.

James 1:26 gives a stern warning about the tongue. *"If any man among you seem to be religious, and bridleth not his tongue, but deceiveth his own heart, this man's religion is vain."* If you do not bridle your tongue and say any old thing, it will deposit in your heart and eventually come out again—and you will have what you say. Every time you say or hear something, deposits are made in your heart. When pressure comes, you instinctively draw from that treasure or deposit and end up producing more of the same. For instance, if you are trying to get out of debt, but keep saying, "I can never get ahead with these bills," you are deceiving your own heart and your religion; you will not like the outcome. Job 22:28 says to *"decree a thing."* Stop seeing yourself as just somebody on this earth stumbling through until Jesus comes. No. See yourself as the one who says it is going to happen and it is going to happen now. God says if you can master this, you can control your destiny on earth. Death and life are truly in the power of the tongue.

CHAPTER SIX

Taming the Tongue and Holding Fast

The mouth of the just bringeth forth wisdom: but the froward tongue shall be cut out.

Proverbs 10:31

God calls this process of creation by words "work" [Genesis 2:2]. In this context, are you working for yourself or against yourself? James emphasizes the importance of taming the tongue:

> My brethren, be not many masters, knowing that we shall receive the greater condemnation. For in many things we offend all. If any man offend not in word, the same is a perfect man, and able also to bridle the whole body. Behold, we put bits in the horses' mouths, that they may obey us; and we turn about their whole body. Behold also the ships, which though they be so great, and are driven of fierce winds, yet are they turned about with a very small helm, whithersoever the governor listeth. Even so the tongue is a little member, and boasteth great things. Behold, how great a matter a little fire kindleth! And the tongue is a fire, a world of iniquity: so is the tongue among our members, that it defileth the whole body, and setteth on fire the course of nature; and it is set on fire of hell. For every kind of beasts, and of birds, and of serpents, and of things in the sea, is tamed, and hath been tamed of mankind: but the tongue can no man tame; it is an unruly evil, full of deadly poison...Out of the same mouth proceedeth blessing and cursing. My brethren, these things ought not so to be. [James 3:1-10]

Look at the bridle analogy James mentions. Why do you put a bridle in a horse's mouth? To move it where you want it to go. When you pull the right rein, the horse will turn right. When you pull the left rein, the horse will turn left. The same is true for ships that use a rudder. The rudder is used to turn the ship in the direction it needs to go. If you want to turn your life, focus on the rudder (your tongue); use your tongue to change your situation. Remember, your destiny is in your mouth. When the rudder on a ship is first cocked, it is just plowing water, but if it is held in place, the ship will eventually begin to turn.

Therefore, if you hold fast to your confession, your situation will begin to turn. If the ship turns suddenly, it will throw all the passengers off; it needs to turn slowly, so as few lives as possible will not be negatively disrupted. The next thing you know, the ship is heading in a different direction. Likewise, our tongues have to turn slowly so our hearts can catch up with our new image—then we can build up a new deposit or treasure in our hearts. This way we learn how to continuously increase the deposit and draw on it until Jesus comes. Soon, you will find you are no longer steering towards "Barely Get Along Street" down by "Grumble Alley," but you are headed down a different path.

It takes discipline on a daily basis. *"Seeing then that we have a great high priest, that is passed into the heavens, Jesus the Son of God, let us hold fast our profession"* [Hebrews 4:14]. Notice, he did not call it confession. He called it "profession" because you are going to start making your living by your speech. What you say with your mouth is going to dictate your life and you must hold fast to God's Word. Holding fast to your profession will see you through when the enemy tests your faith. He will bring about circumstances to try to take you down. It is vital that you keep the rudder in place and make a decision in advance about what you will say during these times. When it seems the devil is putting extreme pressure on you, your breakthrough is right at the door. He puts it on you because he knows you are about to testify. You have to hold fast and be patient with the turning process.

Too many church folks miss this point because they are too "sensory-oriented" as opposed to walking by faith. They have to immediately see, touch, hear, and feel the process. Even though, at first, it appears nothing is happening, plow that water. I discovered that it will begin turning ever so slightly and if you are not watching your compass, you may not even notice the movement.

When asked if she had a job, my wife answered, "Yes," because the transaction had been done in the spirit. She was following instructions: *"Let us hold fast the profession of our faith without wavering; (for he is faithful that promised)"* [Hebrews 10:23]. We know that *"faith is the substance of things hoped for, the evidence of things not seen"* [Hebrews 11:1]. Hope is the goal and faith goes to work to meet that goal. Faith cannot work without hope, and hope cannot benefit you without faith.

Remember, you have Jesus as your High Priest in heaven. He is making sure what you have petitioned of the Father, and what you have confessed with your mouth, you will get. *"Holy brethren, partakers of the heavenly calling, consider the Apostle and High Priest of our profession, Christ Jesus"* [Hebrews 3:1]. Jesus is seated beside the Father to make sure your requests are answered. Sometimes your request may be so scrambled that He must unscramble it before He presents it to the Father. Once presented, the Father immediately assigns angels to your case and the Holy Spirit moves on your behalf. There is a lot happening in spiritual transactions and you have to hold fast.

Another benefit to holding fast is *"...the trying of your faith worketh patience"* [James 1:3]. Being patient does not mean "sitting on the dock of the bay watching the tide roll away." Patience means not being moved from your position of faith despite contrary circumstances. *"But let patience have her perfect work, that ye may be perfect and entire, wanting nothing"* [James 1:4]. Notice, *"wanting nothing."* You can stand on the Word and strip the devil of everything he has, but it takes patience and wisdom to do this.

If any of you lack wisdom, let him ask of God, that giveth to all men liberally, and upbraideth not; and it shall be given him. But let him ask in faith, nothing wavering. For he that wavereth is like a wave of the sea driven with the wind and tossed. For let not that man think that he shall receive any thing of the Lord. A double minded man is unstable in all his ways. [James 1:5-8]

The enemy is constantly plotting to shake you and rob you of your faith. Whenever the Word of faith is sown, he is waiting in the wings to steal it. The Bible says he comes five ways: 1) through affliction; 2) through persecution; 3) through the cares of this world; 4) through deceitfulness of riches; and 5) through lust of other things [Mark 4:15-19]. Anytime you go to church or elsewhere and get a good word, and the devil knows it, he immediately tries to come and dig it up and he will use anybody and anything to do it—family, friends, co-workers, or the media. When God's Word takes root, it will change your inner image, and when your image is changed, nothing can stop you from receiving from God.

About six months after I married my wife, Veronica, and the honeymoon phase wore off, I started looking at her funny. I became very critical and "thought attacks" began even though I was saved. I began to wonder if the Lord really told me to marry her. I started trying to figure out how I was going to get out of this. The enemy was busy planting thoughts in my mind: "Well she can't cook like she said she could. You thought she had this together and that together. But she ain't got it together. See, you have grounds to walk on out of here." These thoughts cropped up even though my wife was, at that time, and still is, a wonderful woman.

When we got married, I had not realized that some things I had witnessed between my mother and father as a young boy growing up in Tuskegee, Alabama had shaped my view of marriage. My parents eventually divorced, but some things they had said did influence my thinking. Words paint pictures inside of us that influence or determine what we see and how we act in life. Pictures like this do not go away until you replace them with God's truth. I first had to understand I had a problem, and it was not my wife.

One night I attended a meeting where a man was teaching the truth. He was talking about confession and how things can be in our lives and we don't even know it; these things can actually control our lives because we live out of the image that is in us. When you are under pressure, wrong thinking is verbally expressed and bad things can happen in your life. So what I had to do was get a prayer confession. I began to confess:

"My wife is a virtuous woman. She always does me good as long as there is life within her. The bread of idleness, discontent, and self-pity she does not eat. She gets up early and gets spiritual food for the house. She assigns her maids to their task. She does not neglect her present duties by assuming others. I thank You that she loves me. She admires me exceedingly, and that the Word is working mightily in our marriage. We have been transformed into the image of Jesus by the renewing of our minds. I thank You that my wife is a wife of the Word. She is a woman of the Word and wisdom is flowing from her lips."

Every day I confessed this. When I first got this confession, I thought I was saying it for my wife. Eventually, I figured out I was saying it for me because I was the one who needed to change. The confession changed my image and I began to act differently. I found out that you cannot move any further than your image. If your image is a bad marriage, then this is the direction in which you will move. But, you can change it with your mouth. Once I got my image straightened out, I began to see and act differently. I'd say, "She's not bad."

Because of my confession, today my marriage is one made in heaven, and I even sit up at night and think about how I can bless my wife more and more. This is the same marriage the devil told me I should leave. If I had changed wives before I had changed this distorted image, satan would have just used the same trick again.

Meditating on God's Word helps you guard your mouth and hold fast to what is true. God had drawn me to my wife, and at one point the devil was trying to talk me out of it.

Holding fast goes against your natural instincts. It is a spiritual principle requiring discipline and faith. Positive confession of God's Word over every situation changes your image and your life. The whole operation of the adversary, his kingdom of darkness, is dependent upon the tongue. However, there is nothing on the earth that is so great or so powerful that it cannot be turned around with your tongue. The tongue controls the entire course of nature surrounding human beings [James 3:6]. But the Holy Spirit can tame the tongue. There is nothing in your life that cannot be turned around with your mouth and the Word of God, including your body, no matter how bad the situation.

Many times the enemy will try to put so much pressure on us we feel we have to say something. One time my wife was shopping and I was waiting for her in the car. She was taking a long time, and it was hot, but I was trying to be cool and real "Christian-like." By the time she came out, I had my mind made up that I was not going to say anything about how long she had taken. I was just going to drive and not say a thing. My grip on the steering wheel grew tighter and tighter and soon, I just had to open my mouth and let it go. That is an example of how the devil can put pressure on your mind.

The disciples grappled with pressure in Mark 4:35-40. They were crossing the sea in a boat and waves began to beat into the boat. Someone once said that it could be compared to oppression or being pressured in their minds. This is how the devil will try to make you say what he wants you to say. Meanwhile, Jesus was not bothered. He was "asleep on a pillow." But the disciples awakened Him and said, *"Master, carest thou not that we perish?"* Fear came into their hearts and they gave voice to this fear when the pressure was on. Jesus did not even answer their question. He addressed the problem and said, *"Peace, be still."* This story illustrates two extreme reactions to a problem: pressure will manifest either fear or faith. Fear feeds the problem and faith overcomes it. Choose faith beforehand, and if you have the Holy Ghost, the anointing of God, and God's Word sufficiently planted in your heart, then it is the Word that will come out when the enemy puts pressure on you.

If you want to turn around a situation in your life, put pressure on your tongue, and turn the situation with the Word of God. Allow the Holy Ghost to give you revelation of how you use your speech. Let Him show you where you have erred and put a "bit in your mouth" to turn your mouth. To tame the tongue is hard on your flesh, and it seems easy when you are in church service or around other Believers. But when you get out in the world, the devil is subtle; he will sneak up behind you when you are not thinking about it, and try to get you to say something against God's plan for not only your life, but also the lives of those around you. Sometimes the enemy will use circumstances to show you something, then he will get your tongue to wagging and you will put it in your heart—now you have deceived your own self. We should build peoples' lives up, not tear them down. The Bible says, *"Let no corrupt communication proceed out of your mouth, but that which is good to the use of edifying, that it may minister grace unto the hearers"* [Ephesians 4:29]. Jesus, our example, never spoke anything contrary to the Word of God.

CHAPTER SEVEN

The World's Word System

> *A wholesome tongue is a tree of life: but perverseness therein is a breach in the spirit.*
>
> Proverbs 15:4

The power of speech is a spiritual law. Jesus reaffirmed this in Mark 11:23 when He said, *"For verily I say unto you, That whosoever shall say unto this mountain, Be thou removed, and be thou cast into the sea; and shall not doubt in his heart, but shall believe that those things which he saith shall come to pass; he shall have whatsoever he saith."* This passage does not say "whosoever shall think" or "whosoever shall dream" or "whosoever shall contemplate." It says *"whosoever shall say." Saying* is one of the prerequisites to having. *Believing* is the other criterion. However, believing is mentioned one time and saying three times. Jesus understood that the problem was not with people believing, but it was with them saying. According to this passage you get what you *believe and say* regardless of whether it is good or not good. Either way you are going to have what you say.

You have to let God's truth come out of your mouth. Even in church, we sometimes miss it when we say things like, "Let us bow our heads for a silent prayer." I have not found in the Bible any such thing as a silent prayer. You have to say things out loud and you cannot doubt in your heart. What can cause doubt? Trying to figure out how God is going to answer your prayer. Now, think about this. When you bought a new television and brought it home, did you take the back off and start taking resistors out of it to see how it was made? No. You plugged it in, grabbed the remote, and began to channel surf. Do you know why? Because you did not care how the television was made. You just wanted it to work!

Apply this same thinking to God's actions. Do not worry about how He is going to meet your needs or bring you out of a situation. *Just say what the Word of God says and do not doubt in your heart.* Simply decide to believe God. Remember, the passage says you must believe that what you say *"shall come to pass."* This means that although the thing declared is not immediately apparent, it is coming. Your declaration of faith initiates activity in the spirit realm. Daniel waited 21 days for his prayer to be answered [Daniel

10:2-9]. The angel who responded confirmed activity first occurs in the spirit realm before it manifests on earth. He said:

> Fear not, Daniel: for from the first day that thou didst set thine heart to understand, and to chasten thyself before thy God, thy words were heard, and I am come for thy words. But the prince of the kingdom of Persia withstood me one and twenty days: but, lo, Michael, one of the chief princes, came to help me; and I remained there with the kings of Persia. [Daniel 10:12-13]

Be patient like Daniel and keep confessing the Word until your change comes. The Christian walk is launched by engaging both the heart and the mouth.

> That if thou shalt confess with thy mouth the Lord Jesus, and shalt believe in thine heart that God hath raised him from the dead, thou shalt be saved. For with the heart man believeth unto righteousness; and with the mouth confession is made unto salvation. [Romans 10:9-10]

The word *salvation* comes from the Greek word *sozo*. It means "to save, deliver, protect, to heal, to do well, to make whole, and to be whole." All of this is the Believer's inheritance. It is available in this life, accessible through faith, not the mind.

In secular society, we have been taught in school to read something with our mind and to believe with our mind, but this is not the case with God. When you get His Word as a Believer, it becomes bread or spiritual nourishment as opposed to intellectual nourishment. You read it and receive it with your spirit; your I.Q. has nothing to do with it. God then begins to speak to your spirit and to teach you at a greater level. God designed this system to give us the potential to believe anything into reality. He has given us a heart with which we can believe the impossible. Again, believing is not the problem. Affirming these beliefs through speech is where we have problems. We do not take advantage of the fact that we can make confession with our mouths unto deliverance, protection, healing, or whatever we need. God's Word is a healer, *"He sent his word, and healed them, and delivered them from their destructions"* [Psalm 107:20]. The word must always go forth to effect change on the earth. This is spiritual law—a law that is at odds with the world system.

> But the natural man receiveth not the things of the Spirit of God: for they are foolishness unto him: neither can he know them, because they are spiritually discerned.
> [1 Corinthians 2:14]

This means you cannot understand spiritual matters with your mind. The mind is too attuned to the natural world's five senses—the things that can be seen, heard, smelled, spoken, and felt. Spiritual things do not make sense to people who are hooked into the world system. They think going to church is foolish and giving money to the church is even more foolish. A person must be born again to relate to the Christian life. The world is in darkness and the world's word system has tried to dominate. Unfortunately, this is the system that initially teaches us how to talk. Even church folk say things like, "Could you pray for my arthritis?" Whose arthritis? By their very speech they claim ownership of a painful ailment. We were simply not aware of what we were saying. How can you pray for arthritis? The arthritis is just doing its job by causing you pain. It is the individual who needs prayer for the deliverance and healing in the Name of Jesus.

The enemy will even use songs to build in us an image of seeing ourselves as low, beaten down, barely making it, or songs that generate more doubt than faith, "Please don't pass me by." This is not from God. Jesus is not passing you by. If you are saved, *"greater is he that is in you, than he that is in the world"* [1 John 4:4]. Songs such as "Please don't pass me by," are simply an expression of unbelief. These things are set up to put a false image inside of you, because unless you have the right image, you cannot have the same likeness or operation as God and you will not have dominion. The devil knows this.

You have to start with your image. Image has nothing to do with how you look on the outside. Focusing people's attention on ethnicity and physical appearance is just another tactic the enemy uses to distract you—to keep you living on the natural versus the spiritual level. *"...man looketh on the outward appearance, but the* LORD *looketh on the heart"* [1 Samuel 16:7]. It does not matter if you are white, black, polka dot, or whatever; the outer man will not help you live a divinely victorious life because satan hates all of us. He comes against everybody to kill, steal and destroy. Battling him successfully first requires the right image.

Developing the right image has a lot to do with your environment and being careful about what you observe. Society has provided so much nonsense to people. It has programmed us to focus on natural and temporal things. It tries to tell us how to think, what to buy, how to live, how to pick a mate, how to be successful, what is right, what is wrong, how to dress, how to eat, and even how to die. The Information Age has brought even more choices, many of which are naturally and spiritually unhealthy. The enemy uses our own conforming to this world to try to dominate us, to breed confusion. Even our young people have been quoted as saying things like, "I don't know who I am!" It is time for us to reprogram our thinking, to renew our minds as born-again Believers in Jesus Christ.

In my own life, the enemy really had me going. He convinced me that my hair needed to be straight and I needed to be taller. I bought some platform shoes, had my hair touched up with "Silky Straight," and "Royal Crown" to slick it all down—all the fads of the era. But the freedom from this bondage only started with confessing the Word of God over my life. Once the truth gets down into your heart, it will remove distorted images and another image will sprout up inside of you. Then the new you inside will begin to manifest out of your mouth and through your body, and you will have dominion.

Re-imaging or re-programming yourself is vital to exercising the proper power of the tongue. A minister friend once shared with me that Oral Roberts once said, "If you get a person standing up on the inside; they are going to stand up on the outside." This principle can impact an entire community. A physical environment cannot change unless the image of its residents first changes. Once this happens, an old broken down house and drug trafficking on every corner will no longer be acceptable. The only reason a community is torn down is because the people's lives are torn down. Inside their hearts, they have an image of destruction. Until that image is changed, all the money in the world won't solve the problem. People need to know who God says they are. Some Christians might say, "Well you don't understand. I've been in prison." That makes no difference. God sees you differently now. "I have been married three times." God sees you made whole. "I'm broke." God sees you with abundance. "I am sick." God sees you healed.

Do not say what the world says—stand against its programming. This includes television. Why do you think television is such a prominent instrument in our culture? The name speaks for itself. Somebody wants to "tell you their vision." They want to tell you what is good, bad, popular, outdated, cool, and boring. But you need God's vision to live life on this earth the way He has planned. The world's way tainted God's plan.

Understanding this will help you rebuild your foundation. *"If the foundations be destroyed, what can the righteous do?"* [Psalm

11:3]. Your foundation has been tampered with meaning satan has tried to lay his foundation over God's foundation for our lives. God's foundation is a foundation that brings people to deliverance, but the enemy has tried to come in and discredit or obscure your foundation and bring mankind to destruction.

The enemy tries to discredit anything that is a foundational truth of God's Word. When the Church was in its infancy, this tactic generated many unfortunate events. It tainted God's plan for the Church with the world's ways. At one point in history, Bibles were taken and put in monasteries or other places where the common folk could not get them. There was fear among the leadership that the common folk would misinterpret the Bible. Interpretation of God's Word was entrusted solely to the priests and civilization ended up lapsing into the Dark Ages. Before this, another unfortunate event occurred. Roman emperor Constantine passed a law requiring everybody to be a Christian. Basically, you had to sign up for Christianity or face persecution and even death. This violates God's way. God says, *"For by grace are ye saved through faith; and that not of yourselves: it is the gift of God: not of works, lest any man should boast"* [Ephesians 2:8-9]. Throughout the ages, this twisting of God's plan for mankind has continuously occurred both in the world system and in the Church. On a daily basis, man began to rely on his own ability, with an occasional nod to religious tradition on holidays.

How does faith come? *"By hearing, and hearing by the word of God"* [Romans 10:17]. So it was intended by God that you and I would first hear the Word of God concerning His saving grace for our lives, and we would say "yes" to Jesus, be baptized, filled with the Holy Spirit, be disciplined, and instructed in the things of God so that we can be used by Him. This is God's way. What happened when a man had issued an edict that everyone had to be Christians? All of sudden, people were signing up only because they wanted to save their lives. This means a lot of people entered the Church, but were not even saved.

Church leaders were selected from among those people, some of whom were not even born-again. So now, you have unsaved people trying to read and interpret the Word of God with no revelation, no insight, no wisdom, and no anointing. Out of this system came false teachings that did not line up with God's Word (e.g. poverty vows). The enemy's plot to put God's people in second-class status became firmly entrenched. And living by the world's standards became the "norm" even for Believers. They learned to live by their senses as opposed to God's Word.

When you line your confession up with God's Word, you enter into covenant with Him, and when you covenant with God, He can come in and work on your behalf. When you line your confession up with the devil and say what he wants you to say, you enter into covenant with the devil. Now, he can come in and work destruction because the words spoken have licensed him to do what he has wanted to do all the time.

When a situation looks bad, look beyond what you can see. It looked bad in Canaan, too, for the Israelites; there were giants in the land. But, instead of commenting on the facts, Caleb spoke God's promise and said, "We are well able." But, his fellow citizens were so focused on the problem they wanted to stone Joshua and Caleb. This is exactly what the enemy will do when you start bringing a good report. Someone may go to the doctor and the tests show negative results. When that person tells people, "By His stripes I am healed," they get funny looks—even from some church folks. This is not about denying that you are sick or being physically challenged. It is about denying that the sickness has dominion over your life by saying what God says about this situation. We must get used to being unpopular and ostracized; this is not mainstream thinking. In our popular culture it is viewed as foolishness. You might as well go for everything God has for you! Make a decision now to believe God over unbelieving relatives and friends or evil reports.

The devil hates this kind of teaching. It exposes his sinister plan to keep mankind in bondage. For years, he has been using our own tongues against us. But once you get your image lined up with how God sees you, and the treasure of your heart is filled with His Word, you can go down the street and just negate the devil everywhere he shows up. You can cancel his work in any community and over people's lives. Once you speak God's Word, He goes to work and nothing is too hard for God!

CHAPTER EIGHT

It Is Well

*The preparations of the
heart in man, and the
answer of the tongue, is
from the LORD.*

Proverbs 16:1

It is important to understand the way of the Word because you might be in a place where money and influence will do no good. For instance, the Shunammite widow woman in 2 Kings, chapter 4, was in such a situation. Here is a woman to whom God had given a baby in her husband's old age. There was a man of God who came through town. Every time he came he would stay at this couple's house; they even built him a little prophet's quarters on the property. During one of his visits, he said to his servant Gehazi, "...*Call this Shunammite...Say now unto her, Behold, thou hast been careful for us with all this care; what is to be done for thee?*" [verses 12-13]. And the servant asked the woman what she wanted from the man of God. She said she did not want anything, that she was content; the Bible says she was a woman of great wealth. So the servant went back to the prophet and said the woman had no children. So the prophet told the woman, "...*About this season, according to the time of life, thou shalt embrace a son...*" [verse 16].

Circumstances were irrelevant in this situation. The husband was old, but his age was not a problem for God. Remember, He had done this before with Abraham and Sarah. So what did this woman do with the Word from God's prophet? She received it, and the same time next year she had a baby. The boy grew up. One day, when he was out in the field and he cried out, *"My head, my head,"* and fell sick. They took him back to his mother and the boy died. She took him up and put him on the bed, the same bed the prophet of God used when he came through town.

The woman went downstairs and told her husband, "I want to saddle up a donkey to go see the man of God." He probably wondered, "Why does she want to go see the man of God? It is not Sunday; it is not time for all night prayer." In verse 23, the husband said, "...*Wherefore wilt thou go to him to day? it is neither new moon, nor sabbath. And she said, It shall be well.*" She could have broken down and said, "My boy is dead!" But she did not let this come out of her mouth even though there was a lot of pressure on her. Then the pressure built and she had another opportunity to say something negative. By the time she got close to the man of God, verse 26 says he told his servant Gehazi, *"run now, I pray thee, to meet her, and say unto her, Is it well with thee? is it well with thy husband? is it well with the child? And she answered, It is well."*

Now the devil will tell you, "You are lying." But the truth is, you are not lying. Now you are conversing in another way and speaking things into existence, though the world has taught us to speak the circumstance. Because we are new creatures in Christ, we are taught to call *"those things which be not as though they were."* We all want to be honest, and since the Word of God is true, when we speak it, we are honest. As a result of this woman's confession, the man of God sensed that something was wrong, because as he described it, *"...her soul is vexed within her..."* [verse 27]. So he went over to her house, laid on the child, and the child sneezed seven times and got up. This was clearly a major pressure point in this woman's life! With this kind of pressure, the temptation to say what you see versus what God said will be very great. But God cannot act unless you say what is in line with His Word. You have to agree with God.

When Lazarus died and had been dead four days, his sister Martha, even though greatly grieved, still managed to speak words of faith.

Then said Martha unto Jesus, Lord, if thou hadst been here, my brother had not died. But I know, that even now, whatsoever thou wilt ask of God, God will give it thee. [John 11:21-22]

Her sister Mary also said, *"...Lord, if thou hadst been here, my brother had not died"* [verse 32]. But then doubt crept in when the stone to Lazarus' tomb was rolled away. Martha says, *"...Lord, by this time he stinketh: for he hath been dead four days."* Then Jesus says to her, *"...Said I not unto thee, that, if thou wouldest believe, thou shouldest see the glory of God?"* [verses 39-40]. Jesus then proceeded to raise Lazarus from the dead [verses 41-44]. Remember, when Jesus started His ministry, He declared in Luke 4:18 that He came to, among other things, *"preach deliverance to the captives."* Clearly, a cornerstone of that deliverance was breaking the bondage of unbelief created by the world system—obliterating the mentality that says, "It is what it is, and nothing can be done about it."

In Mark 5:22-23, it says, *"And, behold, there cometh one of the rulers of the synagogue, Jairus by name; and when he saw him, he fell at his feet, And besought him greatly, saying, My little daughter lieth at the point of death: I pray thee, come and lay thy hands on her, that she may be healed; and she shall live."*

Here we have a ruler of the synagogue asking Jesus for help and he did it by making a positive confession; *"she shall live."*

Jesus was not popular with the religious leaders, but Jairus strayed away from the camp to have his needs met. Verses 24-26 says, *"And Jesus went with him; and much people followed him, and thronged him. And a certain woman, which had an issue of blood twelve years, and had suffered many things of many physicians, and had spent all that she had, and was nothing bettered, but rather grew worse."*

There is a place to go where money will not help you. If you have the Word, you can get help—the Word will give you total deliverance. The Bible goes on to say in verses 27-29, *"When she had heard of Jesus, came in the press behind, and touched His garment. For she said, If I may touch but his clothes, I shall be whole. And straightway the fountain of her blood was dried up; and she felt in her body that she was healed of that plague."*

You will notice she "said" something that lined up with the Word of God. To the natural mind, this might seem foolish. How can touching someone's clothing result in healing? But this woman did not think nor ponder, wonder, or debate. She did not consult with her friends. She said something. Proverbs 12:13 says, *"The wicked is snared by the transgression of his lips: but the just shall come out of trouble."* In other words, a man's mouth shall deliver him, so it was with this woman. In Mark 5:34, Jesus said to her, *"... Daughter, thy faith hath made thee whole; go in peace, and be whole of thy plague."* Matthew 9:22 notes, *"...And the woman was made whole from that hour."*

Then Jesus turned his attention back to Jairus' daughter. *"While he yet spake, there came from the ruler of the synagogue's house certain which said, Thy daughter is dead: why troublest thou the Master any further?"* [Mark 5:35]. Money will not help when you get to this place. But in verse 36, it says, *"As soon as Jesus heard the word that was spoken, he saith unto the ruler of the synagogue, Be not afraid, only believe"* [verse 36].

Fear is the number one tool the devil will use on you. He will hold a sales presentation in front of you, not in the natural, but in your mind. He will say, "Alright, what kind of sickness do you have?" And you will have a symptom of that sickness. Then the enemy flips the page on the flipchart and ask, "Do you believe you have such and such illness?" You will say, "No, I don't have that." Then he will go back to the flipchart again and say, "Okay, how about this disease? Do you believe you have this one?" You will say, "No, no one in my family has anything like that." So the enemy flips the chart yet again saying, "Now you know you have this one because your daddy had it, right?" That is how the enemy will work with your mind. He will flip the chart until you start to buy something he is saying. He is a salesman. He is trying to take your eyes off the Word and put it on your circumstances.

Jesus dealt with the fear issue before He even got to Jairus' house telling Jairus, on the way, "*Be not afraid, only believe.*" And when He did get to the house, He would let no one follow Him in except for Peter, James, and John, the brother of James [verse 37]. Already, a crowd of mourners inside were weeping and wailing greatly, but Jesus said, *"...Why make ye this ado, and weep? the damsel is not dead, but sleepeth"* [verse 39]. The people stopped crying and started laughing at Jesus, but He wasn't moved by this. He put them all out, brought in the girl's parents, and told the child to arise. She immediately got up and walked and Jesus told them to give her something to eat. Notice, Jesus did not decide what to do or say based on what people around Him said or how they reacted to Him. He only listened to the Father.

It is important to understand that God did not kill the child, so don't put that on God. If God had taken her, would Jesus have raised her up? No. The devil took her. He will disguise things to make it look like God did it. This is to confuse people, to tempt them to say things contrary to what God says. But God loves you and has devised a system to help you overcome all adversity. You open the door to this system with a believing heart, and a mouth that says what God says.

Remember when Peter was walking on the water? Jesus told him to "Come." So Peter got out of the boat and started walking. He probably looked back one time and waved because there was a lot of unbelief in that boat. But the Word has enough power to bring itself to pass. In order to see this, we have to change our paradigms. Peter understood this and walked on water—totally contrary to all natural law; He was defying gravity. Then the waves came up around him and Peter looked away from the Word and looked at his circumstances. At that point, he went down to the level of the unbelievers. You have to watch out for this tactic. The enemy will not do something that is lightweight. He will try to frighten you with sudden pressure. But the Word will buffer you and cause you to operate supernaturally. Don't ever try to bring the Word back down to your logic. If you do this, you will short-circuit it and end up sinking. Understand the Word will take you up into a realm above every force on earth. It will take you up there and keep you up there as long as the Word is in your heart and in your mouth.

CHAPTER NINE

Praying With Power

*Death and life are
in the power of the
tongue: and they that
love it shall eat the fruit
thereof.*

Proverbs 18:21

When we pray, God only deals with the answer. Some people come before God and try to tell Him all their problems. God knows the problem. He never told us to pray about what is wrong in our lives. He told us to pray for our desires, and when we pray, believe we receive them (the things we desire), and we shall have them. The idea is to keep the answer before you—the answer brings faith. Why? Because the answer is the Word of God. Always respond to every situation with the Word of God. Praying the problem is a way of meditating on it and embedding it into your heart. When this happens, you end up thinking about your trouble, talking about it to yourself and others. You want the answer deposited in your heart, not the problem. Get your mind, heart, and eyes focused on the answer. The answer will soon manifest and bring the problem to nought.

Does your prayer life line up with the Word of God? If not, what is the source of your prayers? Are they conceived in your mind and then verbalized? Are they a laundry list of complaints and wants? Prayer is simply communication with God. If you are praying words that are conceived solely in your mind instead of from a heart inclined towards God and that has meditated on His Word, your prayers will not yield the desired results. God watches over His Word to perform it. So, if you aren't praying His Word, He can't respond. Prayers from the mind are "psychic prayers."

We have all heard of the "Psychic Hotline." Well, it is the same principle at work with psychic prayers. Words that do not line up with God's Word give demons license to work on bringing those words to pass. This same concept initiates sorcery, and demons enforce sorcery. For instance, a person might declare another person is going to be his or her spouse. They begin praying "mind control prayers" over that person. By doing this, they are sending out spirits that work oppression on that person's mind.

Finally, praying with power does not mean you have to elevate your voice, pray in a certain environment or position, or pray for a certain amount of time. When God said "Light be" and there was light, the power to create and bring light into manifestation existed in the words He spoke. The power is in His Word. Therefore, your prayers must line up with God's Word. You must say what God says. So, if you want to pray with power and get results, you must pray God's Word.

CHAPTER TEN

Divine Gag Orders

Whoso keepeth his mouth and his tongue keepeth his soul from troubles.

Proverbs 21:23

Since there is a time and season for every purpose under the heaven [Ecclesiastes 3:1], there is a time to be silent. The world says "silence is golden," but the Bible teaches that it can also be wisdom. Has the Holy Ghost ever told you to be quiet? We often speak out of the soulish part of our being (mind, will, emotions). If your soul is not governed by your spirit as fed by the Word of God, you need to be quiet at certain critical points in your life.

Zacharias, father of John the Baptist, was protected from his tongue when God silenced him. Zacharias and his wife Elisabeth were elderly and had no children. One day, an angel appeared to Zacharias and said:

> Thy wife Elisabeth shall bear thee a son, and thou shalt call his name John...And Zacharias said unto the angel, Whereby shall I know this? for I am an old man, and my wife well stricken in years. And the angel answering said unto him, I am Gabriel, that stand in the presence of God; and am sent to speak unto thee, and to shew thee these glad tidings. And, behold, thou shalt be dumb, and not able to speak, until the day that these things shall be performed, because thou believest not my words, which shall be fulfilled in their season. [Luke 1:13, 18-20]

Jesus understood the power of silence. He said not a word after His arrest when He was taken before Herod. [See Luke 23:8-9] The Son of God did not respond to His accuser although He was under extreme pressure, facing false accusations, physical assaults, and harassment.

The Bible says, *"He that keepeth his mouth keepeth his life: but he that openeth wide his lips shall have destruction"* [Proverbs 13:3]. David said in Psalm 39:1, *"...I will take heed to my ways, that I sin not with my tongue: I will keep my mouth with a bridle, while the wicked is before me."* This is sound advice because satan is waiting on our words. He will try to push a button to make you look at your husband or wife a certain way and then make a negative comment. The Bible says *"when you have a wrong thought, put your hand over your mouth"* [Proverbs 30:32]. Frankly, some people simply talk too much; they tell everything they think about. The Bible also says "A fool tells all that is on his mind" [Proverbs 29:11 paraphrased]. People need to button their lips because most times their problem is just one inch below their nose. As you begin to grasp God's teaching on the power of the tongue, just make a decision that there are some things you will not say anymore. If it is not edifying, if it is not good, if it is not right or in line with scripture, don't say it.

The devil will try to come and put pressure on you and make you say it. He will try to focus your attention on other people's behavior instead of your own. He will say, "Look how he is acting. Why don't you just give him a piece of your mind? Just curse him once and you'll feel better." This is when you bridle your tongue. In these situations, what helps you is to walk in agape love and that takes faith.

Satan is called the prince of the power of the air. Prince means ruler, and he is loose on the earth. The Bible says, *"...your adversary the devil, as a roaring lion, walketh about, seeking whom he may devour"* [1 Peter 5:8]. The devil was defeated when Jesus died on the cross and rose again. His only power is the power to deceive. He has no real power, because if he did, he would not have to deceive. The devil is all bad. God is all good. Therefore, unless you have control of your tongue, satan can dominate your life and cause you to have a miserable existence on earth.

CHAPTER ELEVEN

Final Authority

The Lord GOD hath given me the tongue of the learned, that I should know how to speak a word in season to him that is weary: he wakeneth morning by morning, he wakeneth mine ear to hear as the learned.

Isaiah 50:4

The Word of God should be used as final authority. That means, no matter how foolish God's Words might sound to the natural mind, remember they are always the truth. *"Let us hold fast the profession of our faith without wavering; (for he is faithful that promised;)"* [Hebrews 10:23].

When the angel Gabriel appeared to the Virgin Mary and told her she would conceive and bear a son and name him Jesus, her final response was, *"...Behold the handmaid of the Lord; be it unto me according to thy Word..."* [Luke 1:38]. She took God at His Word and affirmed it by her words. This was a young Jewish woman betrothed to Joseph and about to become impregnated by the Holy Ghost. In the world system of that day, she at the worst could have faced stoning under Jewish law, or at the least public ridicule and alienation. But thank God she received His Word, stood on it, and brought forth the Savior of the world!

Clearly God has designed His Word to deliver us. We have to make sure we have the Word of God as opposed to the word of somebody else. Just because some professional said it, does not make it true. It may be fact, but still not true. Anything that does not agree with God's Word is a lie. The only question to ask is, "Did the information I receive agree with the Word of God?" If not, let it go. People often use the expression, "Well, you know what they always say." However, if "they" are not saying what the Word of God says, do not repeat it.

Words that someone believes and speaks get deposited into their hearts and the wrong words can do a lot of damage to us. The words we speak do not go away. They live on. Jesus says, *"It is the spirit that quickeneth; the flesh profiteth nothing: the words that I speak unto you, they are spirit, and they are life"* [John 6:63]. *Quickeneth* means "to make alive." Also, the natural things are controlled by the more powerful world of the spirit. In other words, spiritual forces are stronger than natural forces.

When Jesus said, *"My words are spirit,"* He was saying His words are not just sounds. This means they do not stop when the sound stops; these words go on. They do something to this natural physical realm. The things that exist in the spiritual are stronger than the things that are in the natural. What you want is spiritual power, because with it you can change the things of the natural world. John 4:24 says, *"God is a Spirit..."* and we know that God created all things. This means the spirit has dominion over all natural things. How does this relate to you? In your life, you, too, are spirit, not just flesh. [See 1 Thessalonians 5:23]

You have to confess your own safety. You have to confess your own deliverance, or someone is going to have to pray for you. Your responsibility is to release the Word of God to go forth on the earth because God will never work apart from His Word.

Once you start believing for God's best, the enemy will try to come in and test, tempt, or put pressure on you. He wants to keep you from God's best. James 1:3 says, *"...the trying of your faith worketh patience."* Your faith is going to be tried, and when it is, you must have something to stand on. That something is the uncompromised Word of God coming forth out of a believing heart. God's Word is the <u>highest</u> and <u>final authority</u>.

CHAPTER TWELVE

Speaking the Promise

Even so the tongue is a little member, and boasteth great things. Behold, how great a matter a little fire kindleth!

James 3:5

This woman approached me once and told me about a position posted at her job that she wanted because she would be promoted. I asked, "Do you qualify?" She said, "Yes." I said, "Okay, I am going to pray for you to get that job and you will have it in 14 days." So I prayed for her and we agreed she had that job in Jesus' Name. Jesus said in Matthew 18:19, *"...if two of you shall agree on earth as touching any thing that they shall ask, it shall be done for them of my Father which is in heaven."* How He does it is not our concern. God can use angels or the Holy Ghost, or wake the boss up at night with a dream. He is God and can meet our needs anyway He wants.

Two weeks later, the woman came back. She had a sad look on her face and said, "Pastor, I didn't get that job. Somebody else got it." I said, "Wait a minute. You didn't let that job go, did you?" At that point, she understood what I was asking. She said, "No. I didn't." I said, "Well let's cancel all you just said about not getting it." We then thanked the Lord that she had the job. The next week, she came back smiling. I asked, "What's up, daughter?" She said, "Let me tell you Pastor, the lady who took the job quit, and they asked me if I wanted it."

Holding fast to your confession of faith without wavering is critical because the enemy will try to make things look bad. When the three Hebrew boys were in the fiery furnace, the devil tried to intimidate them even more by making the furnace seven times hotter. But they held fast and came out victorious. In these situations, your mind will tell you all kinds of things, but keep confessing God's truth. Ignore what your head says and rely on God's Word in your heart.

We have a God who is able to deliver us, and He has a million ways to do it. When you try to figure out how, you lock God out and you create doubt. Once the cerebral thing gets going, disbelief and fear pop in; then comes pressure, and faith does not work the way it should. Keep your mind out of it and just say, "Thank you, God, your Word says, *'Many are the afflictions of the righteous, but the Lord shall deliver them out of them all.'* Your Word says, *'The angel of the Lord encamps around them that fear Him and deliver them.'* Your Word says, *'The seed of the righteous shall be delivered.'* Your Word says, *'You will never let me be ashamed.'"* Our job is to believe that He will do His job. Stay with the Word; hold onto it and do not let go. Jesus said, *"Heaven and earth shall pass away: but my words shall not pass away"* [Mark 13:31].

If you learn this, then you can govern this earth. Remember, words govern this earth. If you speak them in line with God's Word, God watches over His Word to perform it. [Jeremiah 1:12] There is not a man or demon on earth who can keep it from coming to pass if God is backing it. God is powerful, and as soon as you release God's Words on your lips, the first thing that happens is Elohim (God the Creator) goes to work on your behalf, which is the creative part of God. That means you do not know how He is doing it. The only thing you have to do is say it. And when you start saying it enough, you will see something start rising up in you. This takes you past religious tradition. This takes you into real Christianity.

This lesson on words and the tongue is one of the most powerful lessons in the Bible. It is the lesson of confession. Under this principle, you are not going to have eternal life. You already have it. The devil tries to convince us that we will get our blessings when we get to heaven. But, we can bring heaven to earth once we understand the power of the tongue. [Deuteronomy 11:21] The enemy has tried to keep this information out of the Church. We had a lot of whooping and hollering, a big entertainment session on Sundays—but no power. The Bible says God confirms His Word. But if no word is going forth, then how is God going to confirm it?

When our congregation was at a smaller, more modest location, I was preaching on prosperity. I was preaching the wealth of God at about a hundred miles an hour. A local pastor came to visit the service and he asked me to breakfast; I thought he wanted to fellowship. We went to breakfast and said a few words and then he pulled out a book. He told me who had written the book and how people had gotten off-track preaching prosperity. He said that I should not be preaching this topic. This pastor was associated with another ministry. Since that time, I have helped him and his friends financially. Guard your mind because the enemy will challenge you and he will even use members of the Body of Christ to do it.

Remember, God is not moved by the needs of people. He is compassionate and He loves us and cares about us. But He has designed His system to work a certain way and that is by the Word of God. God cannot move on anything except His Word. People try to get Him to move on a whole lot of other things, but it is tough for God to get outside of His Word. Why? Because He made His Word the basis for His system to operate.

When you are tested, rely on Philippians 4:13 that says, *"I can do all things through Christ which strengtheneth me."* When you're afraid, meditate *"And the Lord, he it is that doth go before thee; he will be with thee, he will not fail thee, neither forsake thee: fear not, neither be dismayed"* [Deuteronomy 31:8]. When you are trying to hold onto your confession and something inside of you seems to be giving way, meditate on Joel 3:10 which says, *"...let the weak say, I am strong."* Watch God come in and strengthen you. That is what grace is all about. It comes with the Word of God and strengthens you from the inside out. Jesus said in Mark 10:27, *"...with God all things are possible."* So if all things are possible with God, then all things are possible with His Word. When God's Word comes forth out of your mouth from a believing heart, it has the same power that it had when God spoke back in Genesis, chapter 1.

Everything around you will begin to change to conform to that Word. Deliverance for your life is always in your mouth, the power of the tongue.

—— ᴥ Conclusion ᴥ——

When God created the heaven and the earth, He spoke words. Those words changed and rearranged an entire universe. He made man in His own image and likeness to dominate this earth and to keep it under His control. We were designed to believe and function like our Father God, using the power of words, to replenish, repair, and preserve this earth.

James writes, *"So also the tongue is a small thing, but what enormous damage it can do. A great forest can be set on fire by one tiny spark. And the tongue is a flame of fire. It is full of wickedness, and poisons every part of the body. And the tongue is set on fire by hell itself, and can turn our whole lives into a blazing flame of destruction and disaster...And so blessing and cursing come pouring out of the same mouth. Dear brothers, surely this is not right!"* [James 3:5-6,10 *Living Bible*].

When Adam sinned in the garden of Eden, he lost control of his tongue. And where he would normally use it for good and to produce life, now *"death and life are in the power of the tongue."* James goes on to say, *"no man can tame the tongue..."* [verse 8]. But the good news is that God can, by the Word of God and the Holy Ghost after we surrender our lives to Him. That's why the devil hates "speaking in tongues" because you are speaking only "life" and things that are perfectly in line with God's Word and His will.

The apostle Paul writes, *"For if I pray in an unknown tongue, my spirit prayeth, but my understanding is unfruitful"* [1 Corinthians 14:14]. When we are born again, not only do we become new creatures in Christ, meaning that the real you inside your body is newly created, but by being filled with the Holy Ghost, our tongues can once again be under control.

Here is something that every Believer should know. <u>There is nothing in this earth so great or so powerful that you can't turn around with your tongue.</u> Jesus said in John 14:12, *"Verily, verily, I say unto you, He that believeth on me, the works that I do shall he do also...."* Jesus used words to stop a raging storm, to raise the dead, to heal the sick, to defeat the devil, and cause a fig tree to dry up. All done with words filled with faith. He is expecting us to grab hold to this revelation of the authority of words, and begin to rule over this earth.

"In the beginning was the Word." Words are the foundation of everything in the earth, including the gold and silver, all were created with words. Remember, words are more powerful and mightier than tanks or bombs, more mighty than the army or navy.

Maybe you can recall when Elisha and his servant Gahazi were surrounded by a Syrian army down in a city called Dothan. What did Elisha do to get victory? He spoke words, and the entire army went blind. Later, he spoke words again, and God opened up their eyes. What did Joshua do to get more daylight as he fought against the Amorites? He said, *"...Sun, stand thou still upon Gibeon; and thou, Moon, in the valley of Ajalon...So the sun stood still in the midst of the heavens and did not hasten to go down for about a whole day"* [Joshua 10:12-13 KJV & AMP]. This is REAL POWER! The power of spoken words.

So, never again talk defeat, never talk failure, no matter how bad it seems. Don't allow the enemy to put thoughts in your mind and have you speak words that will work against you rather than for you. True, the enemy can put thoughts in your mind, however, if you refuse to put those thoughts into words, they will die unborn.

Our lips are taking God's place in the earth. We are His sons and daughters, sent to release His ability and to establish His

Kingdom. How? By speaking His words. For He says, *"...for I am alert and active, watching over My word to perform it"* [Jeremiah 1:12 *AMP*].

William (Bill) Samuel Winston

Bill Winston is the visionary founder and pastor of **Living Word Christian Center**, a 20,000-member church in Forest Park, Illinois and **Living Word Christian Center - Tuskegee** in Tuskegee, Alabama.

He is also founder and president of **Bill Winston Ministries**, a partnership-based outreach ministry that shares the gospel through television, radio, and the internet; the nationally accredited **Joseph Business School** which has partnership locations on five continents and an online program; the **Living Word School of Ministry and Missions**; and **Faith Ministries Alliance (FMA)**, an organization of over 800 churches and ministries under his spiritual covering in the United States and other countries.

The ministry owns and operates two shopping malls, **Forest Park Plaza**, in Forest Park, Illinois and **Washington Plaza** in Tuskegee. Bill Winston is also the founder and CEO of **Golden Eagle Aviation**, a fixed based operator (FBO) at the historic Moton Field in Tuskegee.

Bill is married to Veronica and is the father of three, Melody, Allegra, and David, and the grandfather of eight.

PRAYER FOR SALVATION AND BAPTISM IN THE HOLY SPIRIT

Heavenly Father, I come to you in the Name of your Son, Jesus Christ. You said in your Word that whosoever shall call upon the Name of the Lord shall be saved (Romans 10:13). Father, I am calling on Jesus right now. I believe He died on the cross for my sins, that He was raised from the dead on the third day, and He's alive right now. Lord Jesus, I am asking you now, come into my heart. Live Your life in me and through me. I repent of my sins and surrender myself totally and completely to you. Heavenly Father, by faith I now receive Jesus Christ as my Lord and Savior and from this day forward, I dedicate my life to serving Him.

TO RECEIVE THE INFILLING OF THE HOLY SPIRIT

My Heavenly Father, I am your child and I believe in my heart that Jesus has been raised from the dead and I have confessed Him as my Lord.

Jesus said, *"How much more shall your heavenly Father give the Holy Spirit to those who ask Him."* I ask you now in the Name of Jesus to fill me with the Holy Spirit. I step into the fullness and power that I desire in the Name of Jesus. I confess that I am a Spirit-filled Christian. As I yield my vocal organs, I expect to speak in tongues as the Spirit gives me utterance in the Name of Jesus. Praise the Lord! Amen.

Scripture References:

John 14:16-17
Luke 11:13
Acts 1:8a
Acts 2:4
Acts 2:32-33, 39
Acts 8:12-17
Acts 10:44-46
Acts 19:2, 5-6
1 Corinthians 14:2-15
1 Corinthians 14:18, 27
Ephesians 6:18
Jude 20

BOOKS BY BILL WINSTON

- Born Again and Spirit Filled (Available in English and Spanish versions)
- Climbing Without Compromise
- Divine Favor – A Gift from God, Expanded Edition
- Faith & The Marketplace
- Imitate God and Get Results (Available in English and French versions)
- Possessing Your Mountain
- Power of the Tongue
- Seeding For the Billion Flow
- Supernatural Wealth Transfer: Restoring the Earth to Its Rightful Owners
- Tapping the Wisdom of God
- The God Kind of Faith
- The Kingdom of God In You: Discover the Greatness of God's Power Within
- The Law of Confession: Revolutionize Your Life and Rewrite Your Future with the Power of Words The Power of Grace
- The Power of Grace
- The Power of the Tithe
- Training For Reigning: Releasing the Power Of Your Potential
- Transform Your Thinking, Transform Your Life: Radically Change Your Thoughts, Your World and Your Destiny

CONNECT WITH US!

Connect with Bill Winston Ministries on Social Media.
Visit **www.billwinston.org/social**
to connect with all of our official
Social Media channels.

Bill Winston Ministries
P.O. Box 947
Oak Park, Illinois 60303-0947
(708) 697-5100
(800) 711-9327
www.billwinston.org

Bill Winston Ministries - Africa
22 Salisbury Road
Morningside, Durban, KWA Zulu Natal 4001
+27(0)313032541 order@bwm.org.za
www.bwm.org.za

Prayer Call Center
(877) 543-9443

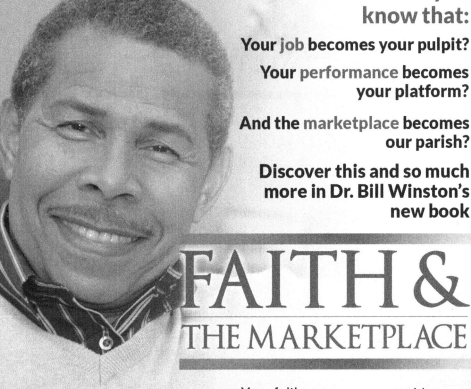